Joanne Harris is the author of international bestsellers *Chocolat*, *Blackberry Wine*, *Five Quarters of the Orange*, *Coastliners* and *Holy Fools*. She lives in Huddersfield, Yorkshire, with her husband and daughter.

Fran Warde trained as a chef. She worked at the Café Royal, on an Australian prawn trawler, ran her own cookery school and then moved into food styling and food writing. She is the food editor of *Red* magazine and the author of three books: *Food for Friends*, *Eat Drink Live* and *Thirty-minute Italian*. She lives in West London with her husband and two children.

THE FRENCH KITCHEN

A Cookbook

Joanne Harris and Fran Warde

Doubleday

LONDON · NEW YORK · TORONTO · SYDNEY · AUCKLAND

Transworld Publishers
61–63 Uxbridge Road, London W5 5SA
a division of The Random House Group Ltd

Random House Australia (PTY) Ltd
20 Alfred Street, Milsons Point, Sydney,
New South Wales 2061, Australia

Random House New Zealand Ltd
18 Poland Road, Glenfield, Auckland 10, New Zealand

Random House South Africa (PTY) Ltd
Endulini, 5a Jubilee Road, Parktown 2193, South Africa

First published in hardback 2002 by Doubleday.
This paperback edition published 2003.
Doubleday is a division of Transworld Publishers.

A catalogue record for this book is available
from the British Library.
ISBN 0385 607016

Photography by Debi Treloar
Designed by Carroll Associates

Printed by Appl Druck, Wemding, Germany

1 3 5 7 9 10 8 6 4 2

Papers used by Transworld Publishers are natural,
recyclable products made from wood grown in sustainable
forests. The manufacturing processes conform to the
environmental regulations of the country of origin.

Introduction

Many of my earliest memories are about food. I remember making pancakes with Mémée, my great-grandmother, in her house in Vitré when I was three years old. I remember making jam with my grandfather in Barnsley, and picking blackberries to make wine. I remember my Yorkshire grandmother's rhubarb and apple pie, and my French grandmother's green fig jam. I remember long childhood holidays on the island of Noirmoutier, going round the markets in the early morning or cooking sardines on a charcoal brazier on the sand, and I remember *poule au pot* in Gascony with my grandfather's old friends the Douazans. So many memories are associated with the tastes and smells of cooking; so many places, so many people can be brought to life using nothing more than a handful of herbs or an old recipe.

It's astonishing how much of our past and our culture is secretly defined by food. Our earliest sensations are to do with tastes and smells; as infants we experience food as comfort, food as an expression of love. Later we make our own associations, but for me, the kitchen has always been the heart of my family, a place where the family assembles, not just to eat, but to be together, to talk, to put the world to rights, to teach, to remember the past, to watch and learn.

My kitchen is essentially French in character. There's a strong tradition of cooking on my French side, handed down from my great-grandmother. My mother, too, is a terrific cook, and when she arrived in Yorkshire – speaking virtually no English and feeling, inevitably, a little homesick – she used the familiar recipes to remember the people at home, to remind herself of who she was, and to keep in touch with her cultural identity.

As far as I know, my father had no difficulty in adjusting to this radical change of diet. However, married as I am to a vegetarian (and with a militant 8-year-old veggie daughter), I have discovered that sometimes cultures clash. Not that I have anything against vegetarianism. I enjoy vegetarian food, and when I am at home I rarely cook anything else. But food is as much about heritage as it is about taste; and the French half of me refuses to let go of so large a section of my past. As a result, this book is a kind of family album, in which every recipe paints a picture, as well as, I hope, an introduction to some of the regional flavours of France.

Cooking is a social activity. My mother's kitchen – and my grandmother's, and my great-grandmother's – was open to all comers. My grandmother sang constantly (and very tunelessly) as she peeled potatoes. My mother told stories.

There were forbidden areas (my great-aunt Marinette's pancake pan, for instance, was formally out of bounds), but for the most part the kitchen was a learning zone for children, a place where philosophies were expounded, histories examined and scandals unearthed. Inevitably, much of my childhood seems to have taken place in and around kitchens. The recipes in this book are mostly French because my main influences come from there, mostly traditional because they have been handed down over many years, and mostly very simple to make. When the ingredients are really good, simple food works; there is no need for complicated sauces or fiddly garnishes. Traditional food demands respect and attention to quality, and this, I think, is the principal ingredient of the French kitchen.

Regardless of other differences, on this subject my English and my French sides are in complete agreement. Food – and its preparation – should be a pleasure. Faced with such a bewildering selection of 'conveniently' processed foods and ready meals in the supermarkets, it is sometimes hard to remember this. There is nothing convenient about bad food. When in a hurry, it still takes less time to make a fabulous salad or sandwich or pasta dish than it does to defrost an overpriced tray of mush. So take a little time in selecting your ingredients; go out of your way to find a really good organic butcher or cheesemonger or baker. Visit markets instead of supermarkets. Rediscover the joy of eating locally grown produce in season, instead of food flown in from the other side of the world. Try growing your own herbs (lack of space is no excuse – even a window-ledge will do). If you are lucky enough to have a garden, then you may already have discovered the difference between home-grown and far-flown; if not, try a couple of life-enhancing rows of carrots or spinach or raspberries or a pot of some impossible-to-find species of tomato. Brought up alongside my grandfather's allotment in Yorkshire, I developed this addiction to home-grown food early in life, and I am still amazed at the number of people who think that tomatoes are round and red and tasteless (as opposed to green and sweet and stripy, or long and yellow and tangy, or orange and lumpy and fantastic), or that most unidentified things taste like chicken, or that strawberries have a uniform shape. Food is a sensual, whole-body experience: look at what you are cooking, smell the ingredients, mix them with your fingers. Enjoy their sounds and textures. Bear in mind that cooking is about as close to magic as modern society allows: to take a set of basic ingredients and to transform them into something wonderful, something from another part of the world. Most of all, have fun. Bring your friends into the kitchen; ask your family to help. Let your children watch. Enjoy it together.

Salads

Many people on seeing the word 'salad' in a cookbook will tend to shudder and pass quickly on to the section marked 'chocolate'. This is because for many years salads have had a rather bad press, and have been associated mainly with dieting and the depression that often follows. However, French salads take us far beyond these stereotypical wet-lettuce-and-celery-stick meals and into an area of vast and delicious diversity. For a start, salads do not have to contain lettuce. They do not even have to contain vegetables, although they do provide a wonderful means of making the most of the seasonal fruits and vegetables that are one of the principal beauties of a French market. Salads may be served warm or cold and contain raw or cooked ingredients, but will most often be served with some form of dressing, usually containing lemon juice, vinegar, oil and spices.

I remember being taught to prepare French dressing when I was about four years old – it's that easy. To three tablespoons of oil, add one of vinegar, plus another of mustard. Salt and pepper to taste, then mix well with a fork. You can use other ingredients to vary the taste: balsamic or grainy mustard, herbs, chillies, garlic or different types of oil and vinegar. The results can be dramatically different; walnut or pistachio oil, for instance, give an entirely different flavour to a goat's cheese salad, or try adding a splash of raspberry vinegar to a summer salad for a fresh, sweeter taste.

The beauty of salads is that the variations are almost endless. Crisp leaves and herbs, sliced fruit, grated carrots, seeds, olives, cheeses, warm potatoes with olive oil, capers and garlic dressing, marinated duck or salted fish – all these work very well, and you can vary your combinations according to the season or to suit your personal taste. They are extremely easy to prepare, and for the most part, very quick, and it is for this reason that I make so many salads, both in winter and in summer. My favourites are among the simplest: raw cep (porcini) mushrooms, thinly sliced and served with lemon, a little salt and a drizzle of olive oil; fat ripe tomatoes, warmed on a sunny window-ledge and served sliced with French dressing and chopped parsley; grated carrots, with parsley, oil and lemon. These are the most basic of recipes, but they can be truly spectacular if the ingredients are good enough, and serve to remind us how wonderful some foods can be with only a minimum of fuss and preparation.

Salads are easy, quick and endlessly variable. Despite being among the most basic of recipes, the results can be wonderful: as good on the eye as on the tongue. The better the ingredients, the better the results, so shop carefully, or grow your own.

I adore this dish. It's so simple, but the flavours and smells of it take me right back to holidays in France by the sea, and to the little goat farm on Noirmoutier where my mother always bought our cheeses.

Warm Goat's Cheese Salad

There are different types of goat's cheese – such as the delightfully named *crottins de chèvre* – but for this recipe it's better to use the *bûche* or log-shaped cheeses. There is a wonderfully earthy taste to good goat's cheese, which, when mixed with really fresh salad leaves, crunchy walnuts and good, spicy olives, evokes the spirit of summer.

Preparation: 10 minutes
Cooking: 5 minutes

Serves 6

300g goat's cheese log: the best you can find
6 slices of baguette
200g mixed salad leaves
50g walnuts
100g black niçoise olives, pitted

For the dressing:
1 tsp grainy mustard
1 tsp Dijon mustard
2 tbsp cider vinegar
sea salt
freshly ground black pepper
6 tbsp extra-virgin olive oil

Heat the grill to high.

Cut the goat's cheese into six $1/2$cm slices and put one on top of each slice of baguette. Put on the grill tray, but not under the grill yet.

Put the mustards, cider vinegar and seasoning in a jam jar and shake vigorously until smooth. Add the olive oil and shake again to blend. Pour the dressing into a mixing bowl, add the leaves, walnuts and olives, and toss well. Put the goat's cheese under the grill and cook for 2 minutes until the cheese is colouring and bubbling. Serve at once on a bed of salad.

Wild Mushroom Salad

If you can't find ceps (often known by their Italian name, porcini), use other wild varieties, such as horn of plenty, chanterelle and morel, or good cultivated mushrooms.

Preparation: 10 minutes
Cooking: 20 minutes

Serves 6

6 medium-sized cep mushrooms
olive oil for frying
200g thick-cut bacon, diced (see the note: right)
100ml white wine
1 tbsp balsamic vinegar
3 cloves of garlic, crushed, peeled and chopped
a sprinkling of paprika
a bunch of flat-leaf parsley, chopped
sea salt
freshly ground black pepper
300g mixed salad leaves
2 tbsp extra-virgin olive oil
6 thin slices of toast

Break the stalks of the mushrooms away from the caps, trim the ends and brush away any dirt. Don't wash the mushrooms.

Heat a little olive oil in a large pan, add the mushroom stalks and caps, and cook for 5 minutes until golden brown. Remove the mushrooms from the pan with a slotted spoon, add the bacon and cook until golden. Then return the mushrooms along with the wine, balsamic vinegar, garlic, paprika, parsley and seasoning, and simmer for 8 minutes, adding a little water if the liquid evaporates and the pan threatens to become dry.

Meanwhile, toss the salad leaves in the extra-virgin olive oil. Put the toasts on a plate, cover with the salad leaves and serve the mushrooms on top with any juice from the pan drizzled over.

A little bacon fried in a pan not only renders fat but also adds flavour. You need good, thick-cut bacon. Don't bother with pre-sliced: it's too skinny. Buy thick-cut from your butcher, or get a 500g piece (I use smoked), keep it in the fridge, and cut off 1.5cm strips when needed. Remove the skin and dice the flesh into perfect chunks of bacon.

Haricots Blancs en Salade: a perfect light meal on its own as well as the ideal accompaniment to more elaborate dishes. The haricot beans have a wonderful, slightly floury texture that is ideal for use in salads: they absorb flavours and melt in the mouth. Don't add salt during cooking, though – it toughens the skins.

White Haricot Bean and Tomato Salad

Haricots Blancs en Salade goes really well with grilled fillets of fish, turning a simple dish into something special.

Preparation: 30 minutes,
plus overnight soaking if using dried beans
Cooking: 30 minutes

Serves 6

2 x 410g tins white haricot beans, drained,
or 200g dried white haricot beans
400g new potatoes
400g ripe tomatoes
4 spring onions, finely sliced
a bunch of flat-leaf parsley, roughly chopped
1 red chilli, finely diced (include the seeds
if you like it hot)
4 tbsp extra-virgin olive oil
zest and juice of 1 lemon
sea salt
freshly ground black pepper

If you're using dried beans, soak them overnight in a saucepan of cold water. The next day, drain them, rinse well and return to the pan. Cover with water, bring to the boil and simmer for 1 hour. Skim off any froth that rises to the top during cooking. Drain and cool.

Cook the potatoes in their skins in a pan of simmering water for 20 minutes. Drain and allow to cool, then cut into wedges. Dip the tomatoes in a pan of boiling water for 20 seconds, peel, cut into wedges and remove the seeds. Mix the potatoes, tomatoes and drained beans together.

Combine the spring onions, parsley and chilli with the olive oil, lemon juice, zest and seasoning. Pour over the tomatoes, beans and potatoes, mix well and serve immediately.

Green Bean Salad with Pine Nuts and Feta

This is a cheerful, easy-to-make salad – *Haricots en Fête* – which my vegetarian husband can eat as a main course without feeling too left out.

Preparation: 15 minutes
Cooking: 5 minutes

Serves 6

400g green beans, topped and tailed
50g pine nuts
200g feta cheese, crumbled
a bunch of flat-leaf parsley, finely chopped
100g olives
4 tbsp extra-virgin olive oil
juice of 1 lemon
sea salt
freshly ground black pepper

Plunge the beans into a pan of boiling water, cook for 2 minutes, then drain and refresh in cold water until the beans are cold. Drain and dry them and place in a large salad bowl.

Cook the pine nuts in a non-stick pan over a medium heat until golden all over. Be warned: nothing seems to happen for a while then all of a sudden the pine nuts will colour very quickly. Add the pine nuts to the beans along with the feta, flat-leaf parsley, olives, olive oil, lemon juice and seasoning. Mix well and serve at once.

Tuna and Warm Potato Salad

This is a fabulous salad for winter or summer, full of different textures and rich flavours. Excellent as a main course – try serving it in a large dish in the centre of the table, with plenty of crusty bread.

Preparation: 30 minutes
Cooking: 30 minutes

Serves 6

500g small new potatoes
olive oil for coating
250g cherry tomatoes
200g fine green beans, topped and tailed
200g tuna in olive oil, drained
4 anchovies, cut lengthways into thin strips
(see note: right)
1 large bunch of basil

For the dressing:
2 shallots, finely diced
3 tbsp white wine vinegar
2 tbsp grainy mustard (such as Meaux)
sea salt
freshly ground black pepper
7 tbsp extra-virgin olive oil

Gently cook the potatoes in their skins in a pan of simmering water for 20 minutes.

Heat the oven to 200°C/gas 6. Lightly brush a baking tray with olive oil. Toss the cherry tomatoes in the oil to coat them and roast in the hot oven for 10 minutes.

Put the dressing ingredients, except the oil, into a jar with a tight-fitting lid and shake until well blended. Then add the olive oil and shake vigorously again.

Drain the potatoes, cut them in half and place in a salad bowl. Pour the dressing over and toss to coat the warm potatoes.

Plunge the green beans into boiling water and cook for 2 minutes. Drain well and add, warm, to the potatoes. Flake and add the tuna along with the anchovy strips and the tomatoes straight from the oven, and gently mix. Tear up the basil, scatter it over the salad and serve at once.

A small but key part of this dish is the anchovy. Tiny fish that are abundant in the Mediterranean, they are rarely found fresh but are instead sold preserved in salt or olive oil, either whole or in fillets. Look out for salt-preserved anchovies. They are less easy to find, but they are the best. Once the jar or tin is opened, store anchovies in the fridge.

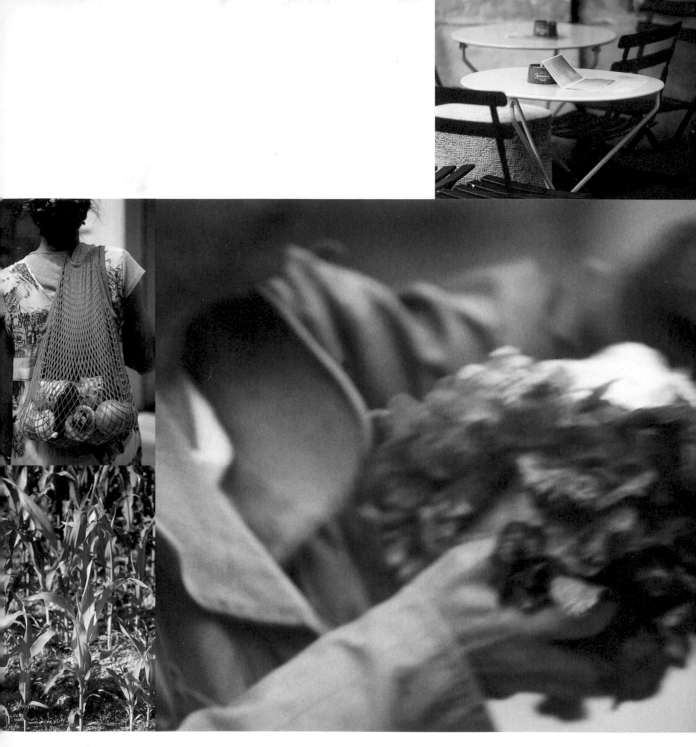

I like to keep an open mind when shopping for food. Markets are the best places in which to find beautiful, fresh vegetables and salad ingredients, so be creative, and let yourself be seduced by what is on display.

Frisée with *Lardons*

Frisée lettuces are one of the joys of a French summer market. As large and curly as a bouquet of chrysanthemums, they have a lovely texture and more taste than ordinary lettuces. The combination of fresh lettuce, fried *lardons* (bacon cubes) and warm, creamy poached-egg topping is cheery and irresistible.

Preparation: 15 minutes
Cooking: 30 minutes

Serves 6

1 large frisée lettuce
2 shallots, diced
olive oil for frying
1/2 baguette, cut into cubes
500g thick-cut bacon, cubed
6 farm fresh eggs
2 tbsp red wine vinegar
2 tbsp Dijon mustard
sea salt
freshly ground black pepper
2 tbsp extra-virgin olive oil

Break up the frisée lettuce, wash and spin it dry, and place in a large bowl with the shallots. Heat a little olive oil in a frying pan and fry the bread in batches until golden on all sides, then remove from the pan and place on kitchen paper. Wipe out the pan, add a little more olive oil and fry the bacon for 8 minutes or until golden.

To poach the eggs to perfection, bring a pan of water to a gentle simmer. Carefully break in the eggs, return the water to a simmer, then immediately remove the pan from the heat. Cover it with a lid and leave to sit for 5 minutes.

Put the red wine vinegar and Dijon mustard along with the seasoning into a jar with a tight-fitting lid and shake vigorously to combine. Add the olive oil and shake again. Pour over the lettuce and toss well. Add the golden bread cubes and bacon to the salad and toss. Serve on individual plates, each salad topped with a hot poached egg.

Artichokes with Vinaigrette

Artichauts Vinaigrette is a dish for people who have plenty of time to eat it – and by the time you reach the tender hearts of the artichokes, I can guarantee that any ice between yourself and your dinner companions will have been well and truly broken!

Preparation: 10 minutes
Cooking: 40 minutes

Serves 6

6 globe artichokes, prepared as shown

For the vinaigrette:
2 tsp Dijon mustard
$^1/_2$ tsp unrefined caster sugar
sea salt
freshly ground black pepper
juice of $^1/_2$ lemon
2 tbsp white wine vinegar
6 tbsp extra-virgin olive oil

Bring a large pan of water to the boil. Put the artichokes in the boiling water – sit a colander on top of the pan to submerge them – and simmer for 30–40 minutes. The leaves should break away easily when the artichoke is cooked. Remove the artichokes and drain upside down to release all the water.

Meanwhile, make the vinaigrette: place the mustard, sugar, seasoning, lemon juice and vinegar in a large jar with a tight-fitting lid and shake vigorously until blended. Add the oil and shake vigorously until a smooth vinaigrette has formed.

If you know your friends like vinaigrette, pour it over the artichokes before serving. Alternatively, serve the vinaigrette in a little dish for dipping. Peel away the leaves and eat the soft nodule, pulling it off the leaf with your teeth. When you get to the base of the artichoke, in one firm tug pull away the hairy cluster (the choke) and discard it, and eat the sumptuous heart.

Fields of this majestic vegetable grow all over Brittany. Break the stalk away from the base, pulling any stringy bits with it. Use a sharp knife to cut the base flat, and peel away a few outer leaves. Plunge the artichokes into boiling water, cover and cook for 30–40 minutes, until tender. Drain them upside down to get rid of excess water, then serve them whole, either dressed, or with the vinaigrette on the side.

Basil and Rocket Salad with Melting Tomatoes

This is a lovely, simple salad in which the smoky flavour of the roasted tomatoes contrasts beautifully with the sweetness of the basil and the pepperiness of the rocket leaves.

Preparation: 20 minutes
Cooking: 10 minutes

Serves 6

olive oil for roasting
200g cherry tomatoes
2 tbsp extra-virgin olive oil
juice of 1 lemon
1 tsp balsamic mustard
200g fresh basil leaves
200g fresh rocket leaves

Heat the oven to 200°C/gas 6.

Drizzle a little olive oil over a small roasting pan, add the tomatoes and put in the oven to cook for 10 minutes until they just begin to brown.

Put the extra-virgin olive oil in a salad bowl, add the lemon juice and balsamic mustard and blend together. Add the basil and rocket and toss until all the leaves are coated. Top with the hot tomatoes and serve at once.

Aïoli with Herbs

Use this versatile sauce as a dip for raw vegetables, or as an accompaniment to grilled fish. Replace the herbs with a finely chopped chilli to make a hot spicy sauce: great with bouillabaisse.

Preparation: 20 minutes

Serves 6

4 egg yolks
1 tbsp white wine vinegar
1/2 tsp dry mustard
2 tbsp water
6 cloves of garlic, crushed, peeled and finely diced
sea salt
freshly ground black pepper
500ml extra-virgin olive oil
a bunch of chives, finely chopped
a bunch of dill, finely chopped

Whisk together the egg yolks, vinegar, dry mustard and water using an electric hand-held mixer or a blender. (You have to work hard if you do it by hand.) Add the garlic along with the salt and pepper, and blend again. Slowly pour in the olive oil, mixing constantly to emulsify the eggs and make a mayonnaise-style sauce. If the mixture is too thick, add a little extra water to adjust the consistency.

Stir the chopped herbs in well. Store in the fridge and use within 3 days.

Soups & Savouries

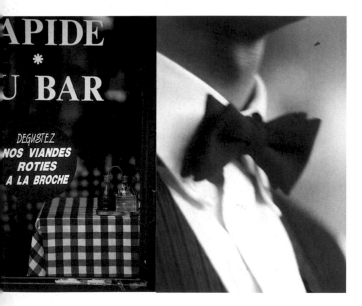

Originally, soups tended to be served at the beginning of the evening meal. There are many types, from clear *consommés* and *bouillons*, which are light and delicate, to the peasant stews like *pot-au-feu* or *poule au pot*, which are hearty enough to make up an entire meal.

I love making soups because they are so easy and versatile, and because of their comforting childhood associations, although a really elegant light soup is also a terrific way of starting a celebratory dinner.

Some of the savouries in this chapter are adaptations of main courses which, depending on the occasion, can also be served in smaller portions as *hors-d'oeuvres*. However, most French *hors-d'oeuvres* are very simple, designed only to stimulate the appetite for the next course. Typically, try selections of any of the following:

radishes served with fresh butter and sea salt
tomatoes, sliced and salted, with chopped herbs
and vinaigrette dressing
marinated olives in oil
half a melon, served with port
grated carrots, tossed in oil, lemon, sea salt
and pepper
charcuterie: a selection of pâté, sausage,
smoked ham and so on, served with pickled
gherkins

The simplest meals are often the best. Try a rich, comforting home-made soup, served with lots of good bread – this is real fast food, good for all generations. Add a bottle of wine for the adults …

Don't be put off by the amount of garlic in this recipe. Roasted garlic has a mellow, sweet flavour, a creamy texture and an irresistible aroma. Roast the garlic cloves in their skins and then, when cool enough to handle, squeeze the lovely flesh out. And once you've conquered your garlic fears here, try Great-aunt Simone's Garlic Soup on page 40.

Gascony Tomato Soup

This rich, sweet soup – *Soupe de Tomates à la Gasconne* – relies on the traditional ingredients of Gascony for its powerful flavour. Serve with warm French bread.

Preparation: 30 minutes
Cooking: 2 hours

Serves 6

400g cherry tomatoes
4 whole garlic bulbs, cut in half crossways
olive oil
sea salt
freshly ground black pepper
200g mixed wild mushrooms, sliced
1 red onion, diced
100ml red wine
2 sprigs of rosemary
1 bay leaf
1 litre vegetable stock
a bunch of flat-leaf parsley, chopped

Heat the oven to 150°C/gas 2.
   Put the cherry tomatoes and halved garlic bulbs in a roasting pan with a little olive oil and seasoning, toss well to coat in oil then roast in the oven for 40 minutes. Remove from the oven and allow to cool.
   Heat a drizzle of olive oil in a saucepan, add the mushrooms and red onion, and cook over a medium heat for 5 minutes. Add the red wine, rosemary, bay leaf and vegetable stock and gently simmer for 10 minutes.
   When cool enough to handle, slip the garlic flesh out of its skin, then add it along with the tomatoes to the mushroom mix. Simmer gently for a further hour – do not boil. Add parsley just before serving.

Butternut Soup

This is a lovely way of using butternut squash, which has a sweet, subtle flavour and a meltingly tender consistency when properly cooked.

Preparation: 25 minutes
Cooking: 45 minutes

Serves 6

1.5kg butternut squash
2 tbsp olive oil
50g butter
2 onions, peeled and chopped
2 cloves of garlic, crushed, peeled and chopped
1 tsp curry powder
sea salt
freshly ground black pepper
1.5 litres vegetable or chicken stock
a bunch of flat-leaf parsley, finely chopped

Butternuts are one of the hardest vegetables to cut. Always use a large sharp knife. The easiest way is to top and tail the butternut, then cut it across into two. Stand each half on one end and cut away the skin from top to bottom. Halve each piece lengthways and remove the seeds.
Heat the oil and butter in a large saucepan, add the onions and garlic and gently sauté.

While the onions and garlic are sautéing, chop the butternut flesh, then add it to the onions and mix well. Stir in the curry powder and seasoning. Pour in the stock, stir well and bring to the boil. Simmer for 35 minutes until the butternut is soft.

Blend the soup with a hand-held blender (a worthwhile purchase, by the way, if you don't have one already). Serve topped with plenty of parsley and a drizzle of olive oil.

Onion Soup

Subtle, smoky-flavoured *Soupe à l'Oignon* is associated with the *réveillon* on Christmas Eve, and is a traditional winter favourite. Alexandre Dumas, in his *Grand Dictionnaire de la Cuisine*, tells the story of how King Stanislas, a noted gourmet, was served such a delicious onion soup while visiting his daughter and son-in-law in Versailles that he refused to leave without a demonstration of the recipe. Dumas describes the king in his dressing-gown, a scarf around his head, tears running down his face as he watched the chef at work. Of course, this may just have been the onions …

Preparation: 30 minutes
Cooking: 1 hour 30 minutes

Serves 6

50g butter
750g onions, finely sliced (using a mandolin cutter is the easiest way)
3 cloves of garlic, crushed, peeled and chopped
25g flour
1.5 litres beef or vegetable stock
200ml white wine
1 bay leaf
a sprig of thyme
sea salt
freshly ground black pepper
a bunch of curly parsley, finely chopped
1/2 baguette, cut into 1cm slices
100g Gruyère cheese, finely grated

Melt the butter in a large saucepan, add the onions and cook on a low heat for 50 minutes, stirring frequently. The onions should turn a golden brown, be very soft and begin to caramelize, which gives this soup its rich golden colour and deep flavour.

Add the garlic along with the flour and mix well to allow the flour to absorb the excess butter, making a roux. Slowly pour in the stock and wine, stirring frequently, then bring to a gentle simmer. Add the bay leaf, thyme leaves (strip them from the sprig), salt and pepper, cover with a lid and leave for 40 minutes on a low heat. Five minutes before serving, add the parsley to the soup and stir well. Toast the slices of baguette and top with the grated Gruyère. Then grill the toast until the cheese is melted. Serve the soup in bowls topped with the cheesy toasts.

To me this bean soup smells of my grandmother's garden in spring. It is a wonderful way to make the most of young, home-grown vegetables if you are lucky enough to have them.

Bean Soup with *Pistou*

This is a light and evocative dish, filled with the tastes, colours and scents of approaching summer. It is extremely therapeutic to make, especially if you make the *pistou* by hand.

Preparation: 30 minutes, plus overnight soaking
Cooking: 50 minutes

Serves 6

125g dried red haricot beans
125g dried white haricot beans
1 tbsp olive oil
1 onion, diced
2 sticks of celery, finely chopped
1 leek, finely chopped
2 potatoes, diced
1 carrot, diced
1.5 litres vegetable or chicken stock
sea salt
freshly ground black pepper
4 tomatoes
125g French green beans, trimmed
1 courgette
4 artichoke hearts
100g vermicelli

For the *pistou*:
6 cloves of garlic, crushed, peeled
and roughly chopped
a generous bunch of basil
75ml extra-virgin olive oil
sea salt
freshly ground black pepper

Soak the beans overnight in a saucepan of cold water. The next day, drain them, rinse well and return to the pan. Cover with water, bring to the boil and simmer for 1 hour. Skim off any froth that rises to the top during cooking. Drain and set aside.

Then make the *pistou*. You can make it by hand in a pestle and mortar, or use a small blender. Combine the garlic and basil leaves until they have almost formed a paste. Slowly mix in the olive oil, add the seasoning and place to one side.

To make the soup, heat the olive oil in a saucepan and sauté the onion, celery, leek, potatoes and carrot over a medium-low heat for 20 minutes without browning them. Add the vegetable stock, haricot beans and seasoning, and simmer for 20 minutes.

Meanwhile, score the skin of the tomatoes and plunge them into a pan of boiling water for 10 seconds, then remove and peel away the skin. Cut into quarters, remove the seeds and dice the remaining flesh. Cut the beans into 2.5cm lengths, finely dice the courgette and slice the artichoke hearts into quarters. Add to the simmering soup along with the vermicelli and tomato and cook for 10 more minutes. Serve with a spoonful of the *pistou* on top of each bowl.

Great-aunt Simone's Garlic Soup

Soupe à l'Ail Simone Sorin is one of the great memory dishes of my childhood. During my summer holidays on Noirmoutier, my great-aunt Simone and great-uncle Jean would come to spend a few days with us. On her arrival, Simone, who is an enthusiastic cook, would often prepare this dish, one of her favourites. However far I had gone into the woods or along the beach, I could always tell when Great-aunt Simone had arrived and was preparing her famous soup …

Preparation: 10 minutes
Cooking: 2 hours

Serves 6

4 tbsp olive oil
5 whole garlic bulbs, cut in half crossways
25g flour
1.5 litres hot water
4 sprigs of thyme
sea salt
freshly ground black pepper
100g thin vermicelli
a large bunch of flat-leaf parsley, finely chopped

Heat the oven to 140°C/gas 1.

Drizzle the oil over a roasting tray and put the cut garlic bulbs on it. Roast for 1–1^1/$_2$ hours, until soft and golden.

Remove the garlic from the oven and, when cool enough to handle, squeeze out the soft, buttery flesh. Put it in a saucepan with the juices from the roasting tray and mash with a spoon. Over a medium heat, mix in the flour so it absorbs the oil and makes a roux. Slowly pour in the hot water, stirring constantly. Add the thyme and seasoning and simmer for 20 minutes.

Remove from the heat, discard the thyme sprigs and use a hand-held blender to make the soup smooth. Return to the heat, add the vermicelli and cook for 3 minutes. Add parsley just before serving.

Watercress Soup

Potage au Cresson is a lovely fresh, green soup, perfect for summer. It's also a great excuse to go out and buy those enormous bundles of watercress you find on French markets.

Preparation: 20 minutes
Cooking: 40 minutes

Serves 6

2 tbsp olive oil
1 small onion, chopped
600g potatoes, diced
300g watercress, chopped
100ml water
1 litre chicken or vegetable stock
sea salt
freshly ground black pepper
a pinch of freshly grated nutmeg

Heat the olive oil in a saucepan and cook the onion and potato over a medium-low heat for 20 minutes. Add the watercress (keep a little back to use for garnish) and water and cook for 5 minutes until the watercress wilts.

Add the stock, seasoning and nutmeg, bring to the boil and gently simmer for 15 minutes. Blend with a hand-held blender until smooth. Check the seasoning, scatter with the reserved watercress and serve at once.

This is an old-fashioned but versatile dish with as many variations as you can think of. Try it with *merguez* and a little couscous, or with smoked German sausage and sauerkraut to add a new twist.

Sausage and Bean Winter Soup

Potage Haricots-Saucisses –the perfect
comfort food for a miserable winter night.

Preparation: 30 minutes, plus overnight soaking
Cooking: 1 hour 45 minutes

Serves 6

200g dried white haricot beans
2 tbsp olive oil
100g thick-cut bacon, cubed
2 onions, finely diced
2 cloves of garlic, crushed, peeled and chopped
2 carrots, finely diced
2 sticks of celery, finely diced
1 litre chicken stock
1 bay leaf
sea salt
freshly ground black pepper
3 spicy Toulouse sausages (about 350–400g)
a bunch of flat-leaf parsley, chopped

Soak the beans overnight in a saucepan of
cold water. The next day, drain them, rinse well
and return to the pan. Cover with water, bring
to the boil and simmer for 1 hour. Skim off any
froth that rises to the top during cooking.
Drain and set aside.

Heat the oil in a large saucepan and cook the
bacon for 5 minutes until golden. Add the
onions, garlic, carrot and celery, and gently sauté
for 5 minutes. Pour in the stock, add the bay leaf
and seasoning, and stir. Add the sausages whole
and simmer for 25 minutes with a lid on the pan.

Add the drained haricot beans and simmer
for a further 10 minutes. Remove the sausages,
slice them and return the slices to the pan.
Sprinkle the soup with chopped parsley and serve.

There is only one way to chop garlic. Place the unpeeled clove on a chopping board. Take a large knife and, using the flat of the blade under the heel of your hand, ruthlessly crush the garlic. Now you can easily peel it, chop it (as finely as you like) and put it in the pot.

You can still buy *galettes* from street vendors in most parts of Brittany, or you can make your own at home. They are good with *merguez* (red-looking, very spicy sausage made from beef, mutton and red pepper), cheese, ham or egg – or even simply with fresh butter – but for a special occasion try these *Galettes Poireau-Fromage.*

Buckwheat Pancakes with Leek and Cheese Filling

Galettes de sarrazin, buckwheat pancakes, are the ultimate fast food. In my mother's home town of Vitré, there is a stall which sells *galettes-saucisse* every market day, and one of my greatest treats was to buy them for lunch. They never made it to the table, though; ideally they should be eaten hot, out of a paper cornet, on a street corner or park bench.

Preparation: 15 minutes, plus 2 hours' standing time for the batter
Cooking: 1 hour

Serves 6

For the pancakes:
125g buckwheat flour
125g flour
3 eggs
250ml milk (you can replace the milk with cider vinegar for a stronger and more authentic flavour)
250ml water
vegetable oil

For the filling:
2 tbsp olive oil
2 cloves of garlic, crushed, peeled and chopped
200g thick-cut bacon, cubed
5 large leeks, sliced
sea salt
freshly ground black pepper
125g Tomme or other hard cheese
3 tbsp crème fraiche

First make the batter. Put the flours in large bowl, make a well in the centre, add the eggs, milk and water and beat together until smooth. Allow to stand for 2 hours before cooking.

Heat a non-stick frying or crêpe pan and wipe very lightly with vegetable oil. Ladle in just enough mixture to cover the bottom of the pan – tip the pan to make the mixture travel and coat the base evenly but lightly. Allow to set over a medium heat, then flip with a palette knife. Cook for a further minute and then turn out. Repeat until all the batter is used. You should end up with about 18 pancakes, even if you have had to throw the first one away. You can stack them up with baking parchment between the layers.

To make the filling, heat the oil in a pan over a medium heat, add the garlic, bacon and leeks, and cook for 10 minutes, stirring constantly. The aim is to cook the leeks until they are soft and any excess liquid has evaporated. Add the seasoning. Remove from the heat and stir in the grated cheese and crème fraiche.

Place a spoonful of mixture on each pancake and fold into quarters to make little triangular cones. Serve at once.

Cheese Fondue

Serve luxuriously rich and creamy *Fondue Franc-Comtoise* with a crisp green salad to clear the palate.

Preparation: 15 minutes
Cooking: 15 minutes

Serves 6

1 clove of garlic, crushed and peeled
800g Gruyère de Savoie or Beaufort
cheese, grated
1 tbsp cornflour
300ml white wine
freshly ground black pepper
2 large baguettes, cut into cubes

Rub the inside of a thick-based pan with the crushed garlic clove. Mix the cheese and cornflour in a bowl.

Pour the wine into the garlic-scented pan and heat to boiling. Reduce the heat to low and add handfuls of the cheese, stirring until all the cheese is melted. Season with pepper. Serve the fondue at once, with cubes of bread for dipping.

Blue Cheese Bake

The French name for this dish – *Soupe au Fromage* – is wonderfully misleading. It isn't a soup by modern standards, but it is an old and very comforting baked cheese dish from the Auvergne region. It's very good as a main course, too, with a crisp green salad on the side.

Preparation: 30 minutes
Cooking: 15 minutes

Serves 6

olive oil
4 red onions, diced
2 cloves of garlic, crushed, peeled and chopped
200ml dry white wine
200ml chicken or vegetable stock
12 slices country-style bread (about 600g)
6 tomatoes, peeled
a bunch of basil
300g St Agur, Roquefort or other blue cheese, sliced or crumbled
sea salt
freshly ground black pepper

Heat the oven to 200°C/gas 6.

Heat a little oil in a pan and gently sauté the onions and garlic for 10 minutes until soft – do not brown or frizzle them. Add the white wine and stock, gently bring to a simmer, then remove from the heat.

Toast the slices of bread. Slice the tomatoes and roughly tear the basil. Rub a shallow ovenproof dish with a little olive oil. Cover the base with a layer of toasted bread topped with sliced tomato, basil, cheese and seasoning. Repeat until all the ingredients are used except for 100g cheese. Pour the onion and wine over the bread and top with the remaining cheese. Bake for 15 minutes, then serve at once.

Pissaladière

I love the strong flavours of this dish, which combines two of my personal addictions: anchovies and olives. Use the best olives you can find – in the south of France there are olive markets which sell hundreds of differently spiced varieties – and those fat brown anchovies preserved in salt rather than oil.

Preparation: 1 hour, plus 1¹/₂ hours' proving
Cooking: 1 hour 30 minutes

Serves 6

6 tbsp olive oil, plus extra for brushing
25g butter
a bunch of thyme
1.75kg onions, very finely sliced (quickest done on a mandolin cutter)
sea salt
freshly ground black pepper
15g dried yeast
120ml tepid water
1 tsp unrefined sugar
250g strong flour
sea salt
12 anchovies
black olives, pitted

Warm 2 tablespoons of the olive oil and melt the butter in a large saucepan over a low heat. Strip the thyme leaves from the stalks and add about half to the pan. Add the onions – it is important that the onions are very finely sliced – and cook over a low heat for 1 hour, stirring occasionally: they should be soft and slightly caramelized but not brown. Season and leave to cool.

Mix the yeast with the tepid water and sugar. Leave for 10 minutes in a warm place until the mixture becomes frothy.

Put the flour and a little salt in a mixing bowl, add the yeast mixture and 4 tablespoons of the olive oil, and mix until you have a dough ball. Lightly flour a work surface and knead the dough for 10 minutes until the mixture is smooth and soft. Brush the inside of a bowl with a little olive oil, put the dough in and cover with a cloth. Leave in a warm place to prove until the dough has doubled in size, which takes about 1 hour.

Brush a baking sheet with a little olive oil.

Knock the air out of the dough on a lightly floured surface and knead for 2 minutes. Roll the dough out to 30cm x 25cm, place on the baking sheet and brush the surface of the dough with a little more olive oil. Cover with the cooked onions. Slice each anchovy into four long ribbons and arrange on top of the onions in a lattice pattern. Place the olives between the criss-crossed anchovies and sprinkle with the remaining thyme. Leave somewhere warm to prove again for 30 minutes.

Heat the oven to 220°C/gas 7.

Bake the pissaladière for 20–25 minutes, and serve warm.

In southern France, slices of pissaladière wrapped in paper can be bought from a *boulangerie* and taken to the beach as a lunchtime snack. At home, serve thick slices of warm pissaladière with a green salad, or serve small squares of it with drinks.

The tastes in *Tarte Paysanne* vary according to the tomatoes you use. Ideally, use fresh, ripe, locally grown ones for the best flavour. Small, part-roasted cherry tomatoes work quite well, but my favourites are the big, shapeless *Marmande* tomatoes you can buy on French markets and which taste so good you might just want to eat them on their own …

Roast Tomato Tart

Tarte Paysanne has a rich, sunny flavour. Make it with the best tomatoes you can find.

Preparation: 40 minutes, plus chilling
Cooking: 40 minutes

Serves 6

For the pastry:
200g flour
75g butter, cut into small pieces
25g lard, cut into small pieces
1 egg, beaten

For the filling:
3 tbsp thick double cream or crème fraiche
3 tbsp Dijon mustard
10–12 large tomatoes, cored, peeled and sliced
sea salt
freshly ground black pepper
4 sprigs of fresh thyme
olive oil for drizzling

To make the pastry, put the flour in a bowl, add the butter and lard, and rub together with your fingertips until the mixture resembles breadcrumbs. Using a round-bladed knife in a cutting motion, combine the egg with the mix until a pastry ball forms. Turn out on a lightly floured surface and quickly knead until even and smooth, then wrap and chill for 30 minutes.

Heat the oven to 190°C/gas 5.

Roll out the pastry and line a 30cm push-up-bottom tart case. Mix together the cream and Dijon mustard and spread over the pastry base. Arrange the sliced tomatoes in the case, season, and scatter thyme leaves – stripped from the stalks – over the top. Bake for 40 minutes. Drizzle with a little olive oil and serve warm or cold.

Quiche Lorraine

This is the original quiche, and once you have tasted the home-made variety you will never want to buy another one again. It is best served just warm (not hot), to bring out the creaminess of the filling and the contrast of textures.

Preparation: 40 minutes, plus chilling
Cooking: 50 minutes

Serves 6

For the pastry:
250g flour
70g butter, cut into small pieces
55g lard, cut into small pieces
2 egg yolks, lightly beaten with 2 tbsp cold water

For the filling:
olive oil
300g thick-cut smoked bacon, cubed
2 eggs
100ml double cream
sea salt
freshly ground black pepper

To make the pastry, put the flour in a bowl, add the butter and lard, and rub together with your fingertips until the mixture resembles breadcrumbs. Using a round-bladed knife in a cutting motion, combine the beaten egg yolks with the mix until a pastry ball forms. Turn out on a lightly floured surface and quickly knead until the pastry is even and smooth, then wrap and chill for 30 minutes.

Heat the oven to 180°C/gas 4.

Roll out the pastry and line a 30cm push-up-bottom flan tin. Heat a little olive oil in a frying pan and cook the bacon for 5 minutes. In a bowl, beat the eggs, cream and seasoning until blended, then add the bacon. Pour into the pastry case. Bake for 35 minutes, reduce the temperature to 160°C/gas 3, and bake for a further 15 minutes. Serve warm.

Peeled tomatoes take on a whole, new velvety texture. Once you start peeling tomatoes for your recipes, you won't look back. Make a cross in the bottom of each one, plunge into boiling water for 10 seconds (a little more if the tomatoes are not fully ripe), remove and peel. It's that simple.

Onion Tart

Beautifully smoky-sweet and delicate, *Tarte à l'Oignon* is perfect as a main course with a summer salad, or as an autumn starter.

Preparation: 40 minutes, plus chilling
Cooking: 1 hour 15 minutes

Serves 6

For the pastry:
250g flour
175g butter, cut into small pieces
2 egg yolks, lightly beaten
beans for baking blind

For the filling:
50g butter
2 tbsp olive oil
400g onions, finely sliced (use a mandolin for the quickest and best result)
120ml single cream
2 eggs
$1/2$ tsp freshly grated nutmeg
sea salt
freshly ground black pepper

To make the pastry, put the flour in a bowl, add the butter, and rub together with your fingertips until the mixture resembles breadcrumbs. Using a round-bladed knife in a cutting motion, combine the egg yolks with the mix until a pastry ball forms. Turn out on a lightly floured surface and quickly knead until the pastry is even and smooth, then wrap and place in the fridge to chill for 30 minutes.

Heat the oven to 200°C/gas 6.

Roll out the pastry on a lightly floured surface and line a 30cm push-up-bottom flan tin, making sure there are no cracks. Return to the fridge to chill for another 20 minutes, then line with baking parchment and fill with baking beans. Bake for 20 minutes, reduce the heat to 160°C/gas 3, and cook for a further 15 minutes, or until the pastry is golden and set.

While the pastry is baking, make the filling. Melt the butter with the oil in a saucepan. Add the finely sliced onions and cook over a low heat for 30 minutes. This long, slow method of cooking makes the onions melt; do not allow them to brown or frizzle.

Mix the cream, eggs, nutmeg and seasoning in a bowl. Put the cooked onions in the baked pastry case, carefully pour in the egg mixture and then return the tart to the oven to cook for 25–30 minutes. Serve warm or cold.

Tartelette Méridionale

A terrific summer dish, lush with the flavours of southern France, as its name suggests …

Preparation: 30 minutes
Cooking: 1 hour 50 minutes

Serves 6

For the pastry:
200g flour
75g butter, cut into small pieces
25g lard, cut into small pieces
1 egg, beaten
beans for baking blind

For the filling:
olive oil
50 cherry tomatoes, halved
1 clove of garlic, crushed, peeled and chopped
100g tapenade, bought or home-made
6 anchovy fillets
a bunch of fresh basil
100g olives, pitted
sea salt
freshly ground black pepper

To make the pastry, put the flour in a bowl, add the butter and lard, and rub together with your fingertips until the mixture resembles breadcrumbs. Using a round-bladed knife in a cutting motion, combine the egg with the mix until a pastry ball forms. Turn out on a lightly floured surface and quickly knead until the pastry is even and smooth, then wrap and place in the fridge to chill for 30 minutes.

Heat the oven to 180°C/gas 4.

Roll out the pastry on a lightly floured surface and line six 10cm push-up-bottom tart tins. Line each tart tin with baking parchment, cover with a layer of baking beans and bake for 25 minutes. Take out of the oven, remove the beans and baking parchment, and set the cases aside. Reduce the temperature to 120°C/gas ½.

Pour a little oil in a roasting tin, add the tomatoes and garlic and toss well. Roast in the low-temperature oven for 1 hour.

Roughly spread about a teaspoon of the tapenade over the base of each pastry case. Top with 1 anchovy fillet, a few basil leaves, the roasted tomatoes and a few olives. Drizzle with olive oil – you could use what's left in the roasting tin – season, and cook for a further 10 minutes.

Tapenade

This is what I eat when I've had too much chocolate. It's lovely to make by hand with a pestle and mortar, which really brings out the scents of the ingredients. It's versatile, too; you can serve it with good bread, as a dip with crudités or tossed over warm pasta, and if you add a little extra oil to the mixture, it makes an excellent dressing for celery or lettuce hearts. You can make tapenade in advance and it will last in the fridge for up to 4 days (if you can resist it!). Add chilli for a change if you like, and see my note about anchovies on page 23.

Preparation: 20 minutes

Serves 6

300g pitted black or green olives
8 anchovy fillets
3 tbsp capers, rinsed of their salt
1 clove of garlic
juice of ½ lemon
sea salt and freshly ground black pepper
180ml extra-virgin olive oil

Put all the ingredients except the oil in a mortar or a blender and pound or blend to a rough chop. Slowly pour in the olive oil and combine to form a paste. Store in the fridge.

Chilli Garlic Bread is my daughter's favourite recipe: she loves both the making and the eating of it. It's easy enough for her to prepare without too much help while at the same time allowing her to create plenty of enjoyable mess.

Anouchka's Chilli Garlic Bread

My daughter's favourite recipe. If the strength of the garlic seems a little overpowering to you, roast it in the oven for a sweeter, more delicate taste before blending it in with the other ingredients in a pestle and mortar. Don't use a blender – half the fun of this very simple recipe is mixing it by hand and getting messy! Do take care, though, with little people's eyes and skin or it could all end in tears: make sure children wash their hands after touching the chilli.

Preparation: 10 minutes
Cooking: 10 minutes

Serves 6

1 medium-hot red chilli
4 cloves of garlic, crushed, peeled and chopped
a sprig of thyme
1 tsp coarse sea salt
175g butter, soft
1 baguette

Heat the oven to 180°C/gas 4.

Cut the chilli in half lengthways, remove the seeds and dice the flesh. (Keep the seeds in if you like the heat.) Put the chilli, garlic, thyme leaves (stripped from the stalks) and salt in a pestle and mortar, and pound until it forms a paste. Put the butter in a bowl, add the paste and mix well.

Almost-slice the bread to the bottom every 3cm and then divide the butter mix among each incision, spreading it over the inner surfaces. Put the bread on a baking tray and bake for 8–10 minutes. Eat at once.

Joe's Potato Bread

This is not a true bread as we are used to it. It is denser, because of the potato, and contains no yeast. It will rise only marginally: don't expect miracles. But it makes a dense and comforting bread, perfect with soup on a chilly winter's day.

Preparation: 2 hours, including proving
Cooking: 40 minutes

Serves 6

350g floury potatoes, washed
a bunch of flat-leaf parsley, chopped
90g butter, melted
2 egg yolks
300g self-raising flour
50g raisins
20g sunflower seeds
2 tbsp milk
sea salt
1 egg

Heat the oven to 200°C/gas 6.

Pierce the potatoes with a knife several times and bake for 40 minutes until soft inside. Set the potatoes aside until cool enough to handle, then cut them in half and scoop the flesh out into a bowl. Mash it and set aside to cool.

Add the parsley, butter and egg yolks to the cooled potato, and blend well. Then add the flour, raisins, sunflower seeds, milk and salt, and mix well again until it forms a dough ball.

Lightly flour a surface and knead the dough for 5 minutes until the mixture is smooth. Cover and leave in a warm place for 35 minutes to prove and rise a little.

Heat the oven to 180°C/gas 4.

Knead the bread again for 5 minutes. Butter a loaf tin, shape the bread to fit the tin and leave to rise for 35 minutes in a warm place.

Beat the egg and brush the top of the bread all over, then bake it for 40 minutes. Serve warm, and eat on the same day as baking.

Three-mushroom Vol-au-vents

Vol-au-vent means 'blown on the wind', and these little pastries should be almost as light as air.

Preparation: 2 hours
Cooking: 45 minutes

Serves 6

For the puff pastry:
200g flour
25g lard, cut into small pieces
175g butter, cut into small pieces
150ml icy water
1 beaten egg for glazing

For the filling:
1 tbsp olive oil
200g girolles, roughly chopped
200g chanterelles, roughly chopped
200g button mushrooms, roughly chopped
2 shallots, diced
100ml double cream
1 tbsp grainy mustard (such as Meaux)
1 tbsp cognac
sea salt
freshly ground black pepper

To make the pastry, put the flour in a bowl, add the lard and 25g of the butter (cut it into pieces first) and rub together with your fingertips until the mixture resembles breadcrumbs. Add the icy water, mixing it in with a round-bladed knife until a ball forms. Turn out on a lightly floured surface and quickly knead the pastry until even and smooth, then wrap and chill for 30 minutes.

Lightly dust a cool work surface with flour and roll the pastry out to approximately 12cm x 25cm. Cut the remaining butter into small pieces and dot over the rolled-out pastry. Fold a third of the pastry over towards the centre, then fold the remaining single layer over to make 3 layers. Press the edges together to stop the butter escaping.

Turn it 90 degrees, lightly dust and roll out once more to the above size. Again, turn the pastry 90 degrees, fold 3 times and press the edges together. Roll out and repeat one more time. Wrap and place in the fridge to chill and relax for 30 minutes. Remove and repeat the above process before chilling for another 30 minutes. Then repeat the whole process one more time. (You could buy prepared vol-au-vent cases, but this is more fun, and the result is better.)

Heat the oven to 220°C/gas 7.

Roll out the pastry to 5mm thickness and cut out 12 small or 6 large rounds with a pastry cutter. Place them on a damp baking sheet and return to the fridge to chill for 30 minutes. Take a cutter half the size of your first one and make indentations in the centre of each pastry circle, being careful not to cut all the way through to the baking sheet. Take a small knife and knock up all around the edges of the vol-au-vent cases to help the pastry to rise in crispy layers.

Brush the top of each case with the beaten egg, making sure no egg goes down the sides where it will glue the layers together and undo the effect of your knocking up. Bake for 30 minutes. While the cases are baking, make the filling.

Heat the olive oil in a large frying pan, add the mushrooms and shallots, and cook over a medium-high heat, stirring constantly. If there are a lot of juices in the pan, increase the heat and cook until they reduce. Remove 6 mushrooms for garnish, and keep them warm. Add the cream, mustard, cognac and seasoning, and simmer for 5 minutes, stirring constantly.

After the pastry cases have been in the oven for 30 minutes, take them out and lift out the centre of each pastry case, putting it to one side. Return the tray to the oven and cook for 3 more minutes, then fill with the mushroom mixture, top with the reserved mushrooms and the pastry caps, and serve.

Even children who won't eat cabbage should enjoy this tasty, hearty dish. As a child it took me a long time to realize that this firm, delicious green leaf and the anaemic white stuff I was given at school were one and the same ingredient …

Cabbage Galette

This is an old peasant dish from the Auvergne region, and although it is known as *Galette au Chou*, it is quite different from the thin Breton *galettes*. It is dense and filling, and can be eaten hot or cold, although I think this dish is best served just warm.

Preparation: 20 minutes
Cooking: 35 minutes

Serves 6

¹/₂ Savoy cabbage, roughly chopped
2 tbsp olive oil
200g thick-cut smoked bacon, cubed
2 eggs
3 shallots, finely diced
3 cloves of garlic, crushed, peeled and chopped
a bunch of flat-leaf parsley, finely chopped
sea salt
freshly ground black pepper
200g flour
250ml milk

Heat the oven to 180°C/gas 4.
    Steam the cabbage for 3 minutes. Smear a pie dish with olive oil and heat in the oven.
    In a bowl, mix together the bacon, eggs, shallots, garlic, parsley and seasoning. Add the flour and milk and blend into a smooth dough.
    Remove the hot pie dish from the oven. Spread half the dough over the base of the dish, pile on the cabbage and pack it down with your hands, and cover with the remaining dough. Bake for 35 minutes until golden and firm.

Fish

My favourite fish recipe begins like this: *Take a boat, a fishing rod, a frying pan and a jar of mustard …* Many people avoid cooking fish because they think it will be difficult, but fish recipes can be as easy or as complicated as you want to make them. The essential thing is that your fish should be absolutely fresh. During my childhood I spent my holidays near my uncle Paul, who was a fisherman, and there was always a plentiful supply of freshly caught local fish. This is the ideal situation, but failing that, it's a good idea to befriend an approachable fishmonger who can advise you and who will prepare your fish for you on the spot (ready-filleted fish loses its taste rapidly). All along the French coast you can find terrific fish markets, and in many harbours you can buy fresh-caught shellfish, crabs and lobsters from the fishermen themselves. It is wonderful holiday food, because most fish and shellfish are very quick and simple to prepare and to cook, even on a portable stove or barbecue.

Don't be nervous of using mussels, cockles, clams and other shellfish. Just make sure they are very fresh – if you buy them from a fish shop, make sure it's a busy one with a fast turnover. The shells should be closed. Sometimes the low temperature of the fridge acts as an anaesthetic and the shells open: just bang them on a hard surface and slowly they should shut, and if not, discard them. Wash them well in a large sink of cold running water. Use a small knife to rip away the stringy beard around the lip. Discard any damaged shells, and any shells that do not open when cooked.

One of the great pleasures of the French coast is going into a café and ordering fresh seafood and one of the dry, cheerful local wines. Muscadet or Gros-Plant makes an excellent accompaniment, though a rosé (such as an Anjou) gives a more fragrant, flowery taste. Serve very cold.

MOULES
de BOUCHOT

2,50 €
Le litre

Moules Marinière

I first tasted this dish when I was six years old.
Like many small children, I was reluctant to eat
shellfish at first, but on this occasion my mother
persuaded me to taste hers. Unfortunately for my
mother, I not only tasted her dish, but finished
the lot, and I have loved mussels ever since. On
Noirmoutier I used to collect them from the
rocks in front of the house, pick the bay leaves off
the tree in the next-door neighbour's garden, dig
for the garlic in the dunes, where it grew wild,
and cook the whole lot in sea water, which my
mother insists is the key ingredient. Serve with
warm crusty bread and a green salad.

Preparation: 20 minutes
Cooking: 15 minutes

Serves 6

50g butter
2 tbsp olive oil
2 cloves of garlic, crushed, peeled and finely diced
1 onion, finely diced
1.5kg mussels, cleaned and washed (see page 68)
200ml white wine (Muscadet works well)
a bay leaf
sea salt
freshly ground black pepper
large bunch of flat-leaf parsley, chopped

Gently heat the butter and olive oil in a large
saucepan, add the garlic and onion and sauté for
5 minutes – do not brown or frizzle them. Then
add the mussels, wine, bay leaf and seasoning,
bring to the boil, cover and cook for 10 minutes,
or until all the mussel shells have opened.
Finally, add the parsley, put the lid back on and
shake vigorously. Serve at once.

Georges Payen's Razor Clams

This is a quick and delicious way of serving
razor clams – *couteaux* – with garlic and chilli,
perfect for a warm summer night on the beach.
At my grandfather's house you could catch the
clams – if you were very patient and quiet – when
the tide was out, and finding and catching these
shellfish was one of my favourite pastimes as a
child, although it took me a long time to enjoy
eating the clams themselves! These elusive
creatures live deep in the sand and come out only
when the tide is high. You have to sprinkle salt
around the clam's hole to fool it into believing the
tide has come in, then, when it pops out – only for
a split second – you have to grab it very fast, or it
disappears again for good. In those days before
computer games, it was a great exercise in
hand-eye co-ordination. Now, of course, you can
buy clams from the fishmonger, which is less
time-consuming (but much less fun). Serve with
lots of warm bread to mop up the cooking juices.

Preparation: 10 minutes
Cooking: 10 minutes

Serves 6

a dash of olive oil
25g butter
24 razor clams
2 cloves of garlic, crushed, peeled and finely diced
1 red chilli, halved, deseeded and finely diced
100ml white wine
a bunch of flat-leaf parsley, chopped
freshly ground black pepper

Heat the olive oil and butter in a large pan, add the
razor clams, garlic and chilli and cook for 5 minutes.
Pour in the white wine, place a lid on the pan and
cook rapidly for a further 5 minutes. Finally, add the
parsley and pepper, toss and serve at once.

Noirmoutier Oysters

Some recipes use cooked oysters, but much more usual is to eat them raw, with nothing but a little lemon juice or shallot vinegar, a glass of Muscadet and a view of the ocean.

Preparation: 30 minutes

Serves 6

2 shallots, peeled and very finely diced
3 tbsp red wine vinegar
24 Brittany or Vendée oysters
seaweed or crushed ice, to garnish
1 lemon, cut into wedges
sourdough bread, finely sliced
Tabasco
freshly ground black pepper

Mix the shallots and vinegar together in a small bowl. Shuck the oysters: place each oyster, rounded side down, in a cloth and hold with one hand. Insert an oyster knife at the narrow end of the oyster, between the two shells, and wiggle, keeping the blade flat. You may need some strength, but the shell will eventually give and open. Run the knife along the inside of the top shell to release the oyster muscle, remove the top shell and cut the oyster free from the bottom shell.

Arrange the prepared oysters on a bed of crushed ice or seaweed. Serve with the shallot vinegar, lemon wedges, sourdough bread, the bottle of Tabasco and the pepper mill at the table.

The coast of Brittany and the Vendée is traditionally oyster (*huître*) country. Cancale oysters are particularly good, but you can find oysters all the way down the coast.

Seafood Platter

If I were to plan my last meal, *Fruits de Mer* would be the main course. To me it evokes everything that is good about food: the joy of excellent ingredients, simply presented; the time it takes to eat, and the pleasure of eating in an informal environment, surrounded by friends and family. This is not a dish to be consumed in haste, or in silence, or in pretentious or intimidating surroundings, or in uncongenial company. It requires time and leisure. It encourages conversation, co-operation, intimacy and friendship. It is the ideal thing for a large and cheery get-together – and even better for a candlelit dinner for two, with lots of chilled champagne.

Preparation: 30 minutes
Cooking: 35 minutes

Serves 6

1/2 litre large clams
12 langoustines
3 crabs
500g prawns (size according to budget!)
1 litre mussels
1/2 litre whelks
1/2 litre winkles
seaweed or crushed ice, to serve
12 Brittany oysters
3 lemons, cut in half
red wine shallot vinegar (see the oyster recipe on page 72)
Tabasco
hearty, dense country bread, thinly sliced

Reserve all your cooking water as you go, and freeze it for a fish stew or soup. Here goes.

Clams: purge them by soaking them in a large bowl of water and then draining and repeating the soaking until no more sand comes out of them. Open as for oysters (see page 72).

Langoustines: plunge them into a pan of boiling water and simmer for 5 minutes, then drain and chill them.

Crabs: plunge them into a pan of boiling water and simmer for 6 minutes per 500g, then drain and chill them. Separate the central part of the underbody from the shell with your hands or a knife. Remove and discard the soft grey-coloured, feather-like gills.

Prawns: plunge them into a pan of boiling water and simmer for 3–5 minutes. Drain and chill them.

Mussels: heat a scant amount of water in a pan with a little knob of butter, add the cleaned mussels (see page 68), place the lid on and simmer for 5 minutes.

Whelks: plunge them into a pan of boiling water and simmer for 10 minutes, then drain and chill them.

Winkles: plunge them into a pan of boiling water and simmer for 5 minutes, then drain and chill them.

To serve, cover a huge platter with seaweed or crushed ice. Open the oysters with an oyster knife (see page 72) and place them together on the platter. Using the oyster knife, open the clams and cluster them together. Arrange the langoustines, prawns, whelks and winkles all together. Place the mussels in a bowl on the platter. Crown the seafood with the cooked crabs and then garnish with lemon halves. Serve with a dish of shallot vinegar, a bottle of Tabasco and a basket of slices of bread. Eat at once with finger bowls and large napkins on the side.

Jean Sorin's Fisherman's Stew

Soupe du Pêcheur is an extrovert, sociable dish, impossible to eat without a certain amount of mess. It is excellent comfort food for the evening after a long, cold day's fishing, with a loaf of really good country bread.

Preparation: 15 minutes
Cooking: 40 minutes

Serves 6

3 tbsp olive oil
3 onions, chopped
3 cloves of garlic, crushed, peeled and chopped
2 red chillies, halved, deseeded and chopped
a pinch of saffron
sea salt
freshly ground black pepper
2 x 410g tins chopped tomatoes
1 tbsp tomato purée
300ml white wine
600g new potatoes
500g mixed, cleaned shellfish: mussels, prawns, scallops or clams
1kg fish fillets: try any combination of red mullet, John Dory, halibut, bream, bass, haddock, tuna, swordfish and/or marlin
a large bunch of flat-leaf parsley, finely chopped

Heat the olive oil in a large pan. Add the onions, garlic, chilli, saffron and seasoning and soften over a gentle heat for 10 minutes. Add the chopped tomatoes, purée and white wine. Bring to the boil and simmer for 5 minutes to reduce some of the liquid.

Add the potatoes and simmer gently for 15 minutes.

Add the cleaned shellfish and then carefully lay the fish fillets on top. Cover with a lid and simmer for a further 10 minutes.

Just before serving, add lots of chopped parsley. Serve in large open soup bowls, with plenty of finger bowls at the table.

My great-uncle Jean taught me this dish – but it is best not to rely entirely on one's own fishing to provide all the ingredients. I always allow for a visit to the local fish market before I begin …

Rich Bouillabaisse

This very old recipe was originally cooked in a pot balanced on three stones, and was a poor dish designed to make the most of cheap, common ingredients. It is almost impossible to make authentic bouillabaisse other than in the south of France, because the rascasse and other Mediterranean rock fish that are traditionally used in its making are just not available elsewhere. This 'rich' version – *Bouillabaisse Riche* – uses monkfish instead, which has fewer bones, but you can adapt the recipe to any kind of fish or shellfish. In Marseille, the *bouillon* is served with a local bread called *marette*, with the fish on the side, and the legend goes that the goddess Venus first made it for her husband Vulcan – to send him to sleep while she disported herself elsewhere. Serve bouillabaisse with lots of warm French bread, and try it with a spoonful of chilli aïoli, a variation of the herb aïoli on page 29.

Preparation: 30 minutes
Cooking: 35 minutes

Serves 6

4 tbsp olive oil
2 cloves of garlic, crushed, peeled and diced
2 onions, diced
2 leeks, trimmed and finely sliced
3 sticks of celery, finely sliced
1 bulb of fennel, trimmed and diced
1 tbsp flour
2 bay leaves
a sprig of thyme
a pinch of saffron
2 x 410g tins chopped tomatoes
1 litre fish stock
600g monkfish, trimmed and cut into 6 portions
6 scallops, cleaned
6 large raw prawns
sea salt
freshly ground black pepper
a good bunch of chives, finely chopped

Heat the olive oil in a large saucepan. Add the garlic, onions, leeks, celery and fennel, and sauté over a medium heat for 10 minutes, stirring frequently – do not allow them to brown.

Sprinkle in the flour and blend it in to absorb any excess oil, then add the bay leaves, thyme, saffron and tomatoes and mix well. Pour in the fish stock, bring to the boil, then reduce the heat and simmer for 15 minutes.

Add the monkfish, scallops, prawns and seasoning, cover with a lid, and simmer very gently for 10 minutes.

Just before serving, add the chives. Serve the bouillabaisse in large soup bowls.

Salmon in a Parcel

This is an excellent way to cook fish so that it stays tender and moist, with a light, delicate flavour. Its French name is *Saumon en Papillote*.

Preparation: 40 minutes
Cooking: 15 minutes

Serves 6

5 sticks of celery, sliced
4 shallots, sliced
a bunch of flat-leaf parsley, chopped
sea salt
freshly ground black pepper
6 x 150g salmon fillets, skinless
1 lemon, cut into 6 wedges

Heat the oven to 200°C/gas 6. Cut six 25cm circles out of baking parchment.

Put the celery and shallots in a bowl, add the parsley and the seasoning and mix well.

Arrange the paper circles over the work surface. Place a spoonful of the vegetable mixture in the middle of each paper and top with a salmon fillet and a wedge of lemon. Close up each parcel, securing the contents by twisting the paper above the fish like an old-fashioned purse. Place on a baking tray and bake for 15 minutes. Serve in the paper parcels, but take care when opening as hot steam may rush out.

Salmon in Red Wine

This unusual combination – *Saumon au Vin Rouge* – makes for a rich, earthy dish, excellent with pasta (serve it for example on piles of ribbon pasta) or rice.

Preparation: 10 minutes
Cooking: 20 minutes

Serves 6

50g butter
1 tbsp olive oil
1 red onion, chopped
1 clove of garlic, crushed, peeled and chopped
100g mushrooms, sliced
30g flour
1 bottle red Burgundy
freshly ground black pepper
sea salt
6 x 150g salmon fillets (skin left on)

Melt the butter with the olive oil in a big, wide saucepan, add the onion, garlic and mushrooms and sauté gently for 10 minutes.

Sprinkle in the flour and mix well until it has absorbed the oil and butter, then gradually add the red wine and mix until smooth. Season. Bring to the boil. Add the salmon fillets to the pan and spoon the red wine over them to stain them evenly. Cover, then simmer gently for 8 minutes.

Lift out the salmon and keep it warm. Bring the wine back to the boil, mix well, then with a slotted spoon lift out all the mushrooms and serve them with the salmon.

Don't discard the wine – it can be stored in the freezer and re-used.

BAR BEL

KARAOKE AU SO

SERVICE
RAPIDE
AU BAR

SPECIALIT
DE BIERI

Rochefortoise

DÉGUSTEZ
NOS VIANDES
ROTIES
A LA BROCHE

A light, fresh dish for a summer by the sea, this Breton recipe, *Raie aux Câpres*, makes the most of the delicate consistency of the skate, the tangy capers an ideal contrast to the fish's rather sweet flesh.

Skate with Herb Butter

This is delicious with Nutmeg Mash, page 167.
Use salt-preserved anchovies, if you can.

Preparation: 20 minutes
Cooking: 15 minutes

Serves 6

a bunch of watercress
a bunch of flat-leaf parsley
a bunch of chervil
a bunch of tarragon
a bunch of chives
1 clove of garlic
25g capers
3 anchovy fillets
250g butter, softened
juice of 1/2 lemon
freshly ground black pepper
6 x 150g portions of skate wing

Heat the oven to 200°C/gas 6.

Trim the stems of the watercress and herbs then put the leaves into a small blender with the garlic, capers and anchovies and whiz until finely chopped. (You could do this by hand, but you would need a little patience.) Add the butter, lemon juice and pepper and blend until evenly mixed. Scoop out and place in a serving bowl.

Heat a large, lightly oiled roasting tray in the oven for 5 minutes.

Pat the skate wings dry with kitchen paper to remove excess moisture, then lay them on the heated roasting tray. Drizzle with a little olive oil and roast in the top of the oven for 15 minutes. Serve immediately with scoops of the soft herb butter.

Trout with Fennel

Fennel gives a spicy aniseed flavour to this rich and creamy dish: *Truite au Fenouil*.

Preparation: 25 minutes
Cooking: 45 minutes

Serves 6

6 trout, gutted and cleaned (ask your fishmonger)
olive oil
3 bulbs of fennel, trimmed, cored and finely sliced
200g Parmesan, grated
sea salt
freshly ground black pepper
100ml double cream
100ml white wine

Heat the oven to 180°C/gas 4. Rinse the trout under cold water and dry with kitchen paper. Place on a large, lightly oiled baking tray.

Lightly oil a large baking dish and layer the fennel with half of the Parmesan, seasoning each layer. Pour the cream and white wine over the top, and sprinkle over the remaining Parmesan.

Cover the fennel dish with foil and bake for 20 minutes, then remove the foil and bake for a further 30 minutes. During the second baking, add the fish to the oven and bake these for 20 minutes.

Serve the trout on a bed of fennel.

Normandy Trout

Truite au Trou Normand is a simple dish that takes on another dimension when the flambéed Calvados is poured over just before serving.

Preparation: 10 minutes
Cooking: 20 minutes

Serves 6

6 trout, gutted and cleaned (ask your fishmonger)
100g butter
sea salt
freshly ground black pepper
100ml Calvados

Heat the oven to 140°C/gas 1.

Rinse the trout under cold water and dry with kitchen paper. Melt half of the butter over a medium heat in a large frying pan, add 3 trout, and cook on each side for 6 minutes.

Place in an ovenproof serving dish and keep warm in the oven while you melt the remaining butter and cook the other trout in the same way. Add them to the ones already in the serving dish and season.

Pour the Calvados into the frying pan over a high heat, allow it to ignite, pour it over the trout and serve at once.

Pike with Butter Sauce

The Loire is a long, murky and dangerous river, broad enough to have sandy islets along some parts of its length, and endlessly fascinating to children. It is there, with my friends Eric and Pilou Imbach, that I learned to build rafts out of river débris, to dive under the submerged tree-roots (swimming in the Loire was absolutely forbidden, which is why I did it), and to fish for pike. The fish were virtually inedible, half bones and half sewage, and my mother was obliged to find all kinds of ingenious ways of 'forgetting' our catch when it was time for me to go home. All the same, it was terrific fun, and has left me with a fondness for this fish.

Preparation: 20 minutes
Cooking: 1 hour

Serves 6

1 whole pike, approximately 2kg

For the *court bouillon*:
3 litres water
1 litre white wine
2 carrots, chopped
2 onions, chopped
2 sticks of celery, chopped
2 cloves of garlic, crushed, peeled and chopped
2 sprigs of thyme
2 bay leaves
a bunch of flat-leaf parsley
1 tbsp salt
5g black peppercorns
a pinch of fennel seeds

For the *beurre blanc*:
2 shallots, diced
200ml *court bouillon* stock
juice of 1/2 lemon
500g butter, softened
flat-leaf parsley to garnish

Place all the *court bouillon* ingredients in a large poaching pan or fish kettle, cover with a lid and bring to the boil, then simmer for 25 minutes.

Prepare the pike: gut and clean it well under running cold water, and cut off the fins and tail, and, if you must, the head. (You can always ask your fishmonger to do this.)

Carefully add the pike to the *court bouillon* in the fish kettle, bring to a very gentle simmer and cook for 30 minutes. Remove from the heat and allow the fish to rest in the *court bouillon* while you make the *beurre blanc*, after first taking 200ml of the liquid to use in it.

Simmer the shallots, *court bouillon* and lemon juice in a frying pan until reduced by half. Add small knobs of the butter and mix constantly with a balloon whisk over a medium heat until all the butter is absorbed and you have a creamy glossy sauce. Do not boil.

Lift the pike out of the fish kettle, drain and garnish with parsley. Serve the sauce separately.

Pike, properly cooked (and caught in less polluted waters than those in which I fished as a child), has a refined taste quite at variance with its troubling personal habits. This recipe, *Brochet au Beurre Blanc*, is one of the oldest and most traditional ways of cooking the 'bandit of the Loire'.

It's no surprise to learn that the pike is nicknamed *grand loup d'eau* (great water wolf). Its large mouth is filled with very sharp teeth, and many people cut off the head before cooking. Order it from your fishmonger, and ask for a river pike, rather than a pond one, because the flesh is white and cleaner. This is for a celebration meal.

Sole with Spinach

I love the simplicity of this recipe, *Sole aux Epinards*: the slight bitterness of the wilted greens contrasts with the melting sweetness of the sole and the creamy shallot sauce.

Preparation: 20 minutes
Cooking: 20 minutes

Serves 6

125g butter
4 shallots, diced
a drizzle of olive oil
12 sole fillets, skinned and trimmed
1kg spinach, trimmed and washed
100ml double cream
sea salt
freshly ground black pepper
lemon juice to finish

Heat a small piece of the butter in a pan, add the shallots and cook gently for 10 minutes over a low heat. Do not allow them to colour.

Meanwhile, set the grill to high. Lightly oil a baking tray and put it under the grill to heat. When the tray is hot, twist the sole fillets and place them in a layer on the tray – you should hear them sizzle as they touch it. Put under the hot grill for 4–5 minutes, then remove them and set the grill to low.

Place the spinach in a large saucepan with 3 tablespoons of water and cook for up to 3 minutes, stirring frequently. The spinach should soften and warm but retain its shape and texture. Put the spinach in a lightly buttered dish and arrange the sole fillets on top. Place under the low grill to keep warm.

Add the cream and seasoning to the shallots and continue to simmer. Cut the remaining butter into small knobs, adding a few pieces at a time to the simmering cream and mixing well with a balloon whisk. When all the butter is added you should have a glossy sauce. Pour the sauce over the spinach and sole and finish with a squeeze of lemon.

Dover sole is superior to lemon sole. It has a firm but delicate texture and an exquisite taste, but with these qualities goes an expensive price tag. Lemon sole is more affordable, but you lose a little refinement in taste and texture.

Grilled Sole with Hollandaise

Sole is a delicious, tender fish which needs very little to enhance it. (See page 93 for a note about sole.) *Sole à l'Hollandaise* is perfect – indeed hollandaise sauce is a perfect accompaniment to all kinds of fish, as well as making asparagus or green beans into an elegant vegetarian starter.

Preparation: 25 minutes
Cooking: 25 minutes

Serves 6

For the hollandaise:
350g butter
2 tbsp white wine vinegar
juice of 1 lemon
6 egg yolks

For the fish:
12 sole fillets
olive oil
sea salt
freshly ground black pepper
a bunch of flat-leaf parsley
3 lemons, halved

First make the sauce. Melt the butter slowly in a saucepan. In a separate, small saucepan, heat the white wine vinegar and lemon juice until just boiling. Place the egg yolks in a jug and blend with a hand-held blender, then slowly add the hot vinegar and lemon juice. Then, just as the butter comes to the boil, slowly pour it into the egg yolks and vinegar, constantly blending until all the butter is incorporated. Place the jug in a basin of hot water and cover until ready to serve. If it is too thick, blend in a dash of water.

Set the grill to hot. Lay the sole fillets on the grill pan, drizzle with olive oil, season and place under the hot grill for 5 minutes. Serve the sole with sprigs of parsley, halves of lemon and the hollandaise sauce.

Simone's Marinated Tuna

Try this great dish, which should be made using only really fresh tuna, with steamed sliced new potatoes and a green salad. One of my great-aunt Simone's favourites, this dish is absurdly simple and quick to make.

Preparation: 10 minutes, plus 12 hours' marinating
Cooking: 8 minutes

Serves 6

6 shallots, finely sliced
zest and juice of 6 lemons
150ml olive oil
2 chillies, red or green, halved, deseeded and diced
sea salt
freshly ground black pepper
6 x 125g tuna fillet, thinly sliced

In a large, low-sided dish mix together the shallots, lemon zest and juice, olive oil, chilli and seasoning. Finally, add the tuna fillets and leave to marinate for 12 hours, turning occasionally.

Heat a grill or barbecue to hot and take the tuna from the marinade. Cook the fish for 1–2 minutes on each side for rare (4 minutes for well done) and serve at once, drizzled with the remaining marinade.

Mullet with a Mustard Crust

Nothing could be easier than this recipe, *Rouget à la Moutarde*, but it is important that the fish is fresh from the sea to retain that perfect flavour. Serve with steamed potatoes and watercress.

Preparation: 10 minutes
Cooking: 20 minutes

Serves 6

6 red mullet, gutted and scaled
2 tbsp Dijon mustard
200g jar grainy mustard (such as Meaux)
olive oil

Heat the oven to 200°C/gas 6.

Make 3 incisions across the fish on each side. Mix the Dijon and grainy mustard and spread thickly all over the fish, pushing some into each of the cuts. Lightly oil a large baking tray, place the fish on it and bake in the top of the oven for 20 minutes. Serve at once.

When I was a child, red mullet were so common on Noirmoutier that you could almost catch them with your hands. It was our staple diet, grilled, barbecued or as the principal ingredient for fish soup. Now these delicious fish are less easy to find, and are becoming quite a delicacy in expensive restaurants.

Poultry

Poultry has always been an important part of the French kitchen, which is hardly surprising in a country with such a strong farming and rural tradition. At one time, every country family kept hens, ducks or geese, and these birds still tend to be associated with peasant dishes. Wild birds, too, have their place, especially in the more southern, mountainous regions of France, but many of these birds are difficult to find in England, and we have adapted some dishes accordingly. Choose your poultry well. It is worth finding a good organic butcher or farmer who can advise and supply you.

The age of the chicken usually determines the method of cooking. Poussin (3 months or less, average weight 400g, serves 2): these birds should be split lengthways and grilled for 10 minutes on each side, or oven-roasted for 20 minutes. The flesh is extremely tender, but has a very light taste. Spring chicken (3–6 months, average weight 800g, serves 4): roast in the oven for 20 minutes per 500g. The flesh is tasty and tender. Pullet (7–8 months, average weight

2–3kg, serves 6): oven- or pot-roasted, the flesh is firm and of superior taste. Hen (12 months or more, average weight 1.5-3kg, serves 4): these birds are perfect for pot-roasting or braising. The taste is excellent, but unless cooked for a long time the flesh can be rather tough. Braise or stew for 3-4 hours. Ideal for country dishes such as *pot-au-feu* or *poule au pot*.

Duck flesh is dark and quite strong in taste. A duckling (2–3 months, average weight 800g) can be pan-fried (10–12 minutes per 500g) or roasted (15 minutes per 500g). An older bird (4 months or more) is better roasted (18 minutes per 500g) or braised (about 3 hours).

Goose is exceptional, but quite rich in fat. Don't be afraid of this; goose fat is wonderful for roasting potatoes and other vegetables. Roast the goose (age 6–8 months minimum, average weight 4–5 kg) for 30 minutes per 500g.

It's best to use young pigeons (3–5 months, average weight, 300g). The flesh is delicate and very slightly gamey, and can be roasted or sautéed (about 30 minutes, one bird serves 2).

These recipes are not designed with mass-produced poultry in mind. A fresh, well-fed, free-range chicken is a world away from a plastic-wrapped, watery chicken fillet. Similarly, different birds have very different characteristics, determined by age, species and diet, and you should bear this in mind when making your choice.

Madame Douazan's Poule au Pot

This centuries-old dish remains one of the simplest and most traditional methods of cooking chicken. Its patron is King Henri IV, who, concerned at the general poverty of his people, declared that under his reign even the poorest family should be able to have *poule au pot* every Sunday. Many people still use this sixteenth-century recipe, and this is Madame Douazan's version, which I first tried at her home, and which I always associate with her.

The people of Nérac in Gascony, where she lives, have a special affection for Henri IV. He had a castle there, with a wild park, La Garenne, where he spent many summers before coming to the throne. Local folklore has it that one year he fell in love with a girl, Fleurette, who drowned herself when the young Henri deserted her. La Garenne has a fountain with a marble statue in memory of her, and the Nérac chocolaterie, La Cigale, makes the most wonderful little bittersweet chocolates called Amours de Fleurette. They're a romantic lot in Nérac …

Preparation: 35 minutes
Cooking: time: 2 hours

Serves 6

1 x 2–2.5kg free-range chicken
900ml water
300ml white wine
8 shallots, peeled
2 bay leaves
3 sprigs of thyme
6 cloves
sea salt
freshly ground black pepper
12 small potatoes
4 carrots, cut into 5cm lengths, or 12 baby carrots
1 turnip, cut into wedges, or 6 baby turnips
3 leeks, cut into 5cm lengths, or 6 baby leeks
4 sticks of celery, cut into 5cm lengths
1 small cabbage, cored and cut into wedges

For the stuffing:
200g lean pork meat, minced
100g thick-cut bacon, diced
100g chicken livers, roughly chopped
1 egg
2 cloves of garlic, crushed, peeled and chopped
4 shallots, diced
a bunch of flat-leaf parsley, chopped
50g breadcrumbs, made from a dried loaf
sea salt
freshly ground black pepper

First prepare the stuffing. Put the pork, bacon and chicken livers in a bowl. Add the egg, garlic, shallots, parsley, breadcrumbs and seasoning and mix everything together. You get a really good, even mix if you do this with your hands.

Heat the oven to 180°C/gas 4.

Trim the chicken cavity of any excess fat and fill with the stuffing. Close up the neck and tail end of the chicken with a poultry needle and thread or by weaving cocktail sticks through. Place the chicken in a large casserole dish and add the water and wine, shallots, bay leaves, thyme, cloves and seasoning. Cover with a lid and cook in the preheated oven for 1½ hours.

When the hour and a half has elapsed, add the potatoes, carrots and turnip to the chicken in the pot, immerse them in the cooking juices and cook the casserole for a further 15 minutes. Then remove the pot from the oven.

Carefully lift out the chicken and rest it on a wire rack to drain off excess cooking juices. Return these juices to the pot, place the pot over a moderate heat on the hob, add the leeks, celery and cabbage, cover with a lid and simmer for 10 minutes.

While the vegetables are simmering, remove and discard the skin from the chicken, and carve the meat and stuffing.

Scoop the vegetables out of the cooking stock and serve them in individual, deep bowls with the chicken and the stuffing, and a generous ladle of the cooking stock.

Poule au pot is a peasants' dish. It works best with an older bird, the lengthy cooking bringing out the stronger flavours. Cooked in this way, the meat becomes sweet and tender, but it is important to use a free-range chicken and good quality vegetables. For maximum authenticity, serve the leftover cooking stock as a soup starter, with vermicelli.

Garlic Roast Chicken

Garlic and rosemary give this dish, *Poulet à l'Ail*, a lovely Provençal flavour, filling your kitchen with the aromas of summer holidays all year round.

Preparation: 40 minutes
Cooking: 1½–2 hours

Serves 6

3 whole garlic bulbs
1 chicken
4 sprigs of rosemary
1 lemon, sliced
sea salt and freshly ground black pepper
olive oil for drizzling
2 tbsp flour
200ml white wine
a bunch of flat-leaf parsley, finely chopped

Break the garlic cloves away from the bulbs, place in a small saucepan, cover with water and simmer gently with a lid on for 30 minutes. Leave to cool in the water. Drain the garlic cloves but don't throw the water away.

Heat the oven to 180°C/gas 4. Carefully ease the skin of the chicken away from the breasts. Place a sprig of rosemary and a layer of lemon slices between the skin and the meat on each side. Stuff the remaining rosemary and lemon, along with the garlic cloves, into the chicken. Season.

Drizzle a heavy-based roasting tin with olive oil, place the chicken on it and cook it according to weight: 20 minutes per 500g and 20 minutes extra. Transfer the cooked chicken to a serving board and keep it warm while you make the sauce. Place the roasting tin directly over a low heat, add the flour and blend it in well. Slowly pour in the reserved garlic water, stirring constantly. Add most of the white wine, bring to the boil and adjust the consistency with extra wine if desired. Pass through a sieve into a saucepan, add the parsley and bring to a simmer.

Carve the chicken and serve with the sauce.

Country Chicken

This is a simple and tasty way of cooking young chickens, and works very well with rice or pasta.

Preparation: 20 minutes, plus overnight marinating
Cooking: 50 minutes

Serves 6

2 small chickens, cut into 6 pieces each (ask your butcher to do it)
12 shallots, peeled
5 bay leaves
400g thick-cut smoked bacon, chopped
2 tbsp olive oil
sea salt
freshly ground black pepper
2 tbsp grainy mustard (such as Meaux)
a bunch of French tarragon
200ml white wine

Trim the chicken pieces of fat and place them in a bowl. Add the whole shallots, bay leaves, bacon, olive oil and seasoning. Mix well, cover and leave to marinate in the fridge overnight.

Heat the oven to 180°C/gas 4.

Transfer the marinating chicken to a large roasting tin, and spoon its marinade over it. Cook for 40 minutes.

Place the mustard in a bowl. Strip the tarragon leaves from their stalks and chop finely, add to the mustard along with the white wine, and mix well.

Remove the chicken from the oven and drain off the excess fat, then pour the mustard mix over the chicken. Mix well and return to the oven to cook for another 10 minutes.

Coq au Vin: part of a dwindling tradition of old French dishes relying on wine, herbs and a generous cooking time to ensure maximum tenderness and flavour.

Coq au Vin

This is another very old dish, invented – or so the story goes – by Julius Caesar. A group of Gauls had been cornered Asterix-fashion by one of Caesar's garrisons. To prove that they had plenty to eat, the Gauls sent out an old cockerel to the enemy, with a message around its neck saying '*Bon appétit!*' Caesar promptly invited the leaders of the Gaulish tribes to a dinner, in the course of which he served the cockerel (cooked to perfection in wine and rare herbs), promising the Gauls that if they surrendered, he would not only give them the recipe, but personally ensure that they and their descendants ate well and lived in prosperity for ever. Did they believe him? The story doesn't tell … Make this dish the night before serving to let the flavours infuse and intensify.

Preparation: 40 minutes, plus overnight marinating if desired
Cooking: 50 minutes

Serves 6

1 chicken, weighing about 1kg, jointed into 12 pieces (ask your butcher to do this)
500ml red wine
1 tbsp olive oil
150g thick-cut bacon, cubed
12 small shallots, peeled
200g button mushrooms
1 clove of garlic, crushed, peeled and chopped
3 tbsp flour
300ml chicken stock
2 bay leaves
2 sprigs of thyme
sea salt
freshly ground black pepper
a bunch of flat-leaf parsley, chopped

Trim the chicken pieces of excess fat. For a really rich flavour, marinate the chicken pieces in the wine overnight. The next day, pour off the marinade (keep it to cook with) and dry the chicken well with kitchen paper to make frying easier.

Heat the oven to 180°C/gas 4.

Put the olive oil and bacon in a large ovenproof casserole dish and cook over a medium heat for 3 minutes. Add the whole shallots and cook for a further 6 minutes until browned, then add the mushrooms and garlic and cook for another 2 minutes, stirring well. Remove the ingredients from the pan and set to one side.

Place the chicken in the casserole and cook until golden and sealed all over – do this in batches to get a good even colour. Set the browned chicken to one side.

Reduce the heat, add the flour to the pan and allow it to absorb the fat. Don't forget to mix in all the coloured cooking bits on the side of the pan. Slowly stir in the red wine (or reserved marinade) and chicken stock and bring to the boil. Return the chicken, vegetables and bacon to the casserole dish, along with the bay leaves, thyme and seasoning. Cover and cook in the oven for 35 minutes. Just before serving, add the chopped parsley.

Duck Confit Tart

Serve this tart warm, with a green salad alongside.

Preparation: 40 minutes
Cooking: 45 minutes

Serves 6

For the pastry:
250g self-raising flour
125g butter, cut into small pieces
cold water

For the filling:
1 x 400g tin duck or goose *confit*
500g small whole potatoes, cooked
4 eggs
75ml milk
2 tbsp double cream
butter for greasing
4 shallots, diced
2 cloves of garlic, crushed, peeled and chopped
a bunch of flat-leaf parsley, chopped
sea salt
freshly ground black pepper

To make the pastry, put the flour in a bowl, add the butter, and rub together with your fingertips until the mixture resembles breadcrumbs. Using a round-bladed knife in a cutting motion, combine a couple of tablespoons of cold water with the mix until a pastry ball forms. Turn out on a lightly floured surface and quickly knead until the pastry is even and smooth, then wrap and place in the fridge to chill for 30 minutes.

To make the filling, open the tin of *confit* and remove the meat (save the fat, in the fridge, for roasting potatoes). Discard the skin and then roughly chop the meat. Slice the potatoes. In a bowl, beat the eggs with the milk and cream.

Heat the oven to 220°C/gas 7.

Lightly butter a 20–25cm pie dish. Roll out the pastry and use it to line the dish.

Add the confit, shallots, garlic, parsley and seasoning to the pie base, then layer the potatoes over the top. Finally, pour the egg mix over. Cook the pie in the middle of the oven for 45 minutes. Reduce the oven temperature after 30 minutes if the tart is browning too much on top.

Façon Bistrot

Les entrées

Pèle mèle de tomates mozzarella au bas
Aiguillette de saumon fumé sur lit de betteraves
Terrine de foies de volaille, compotée d'oignons
...tait de melon et JAMBON d'AOSTE au myrtil

This is one of those magical out-of-the-
storecupboard dishes – that is, so long as you buy
tins of *confit* when you are in France. The dish is
straightforward to make and delicious to eat, and
you can hunt down tins of *confit* in this country too.

Crunchy Roast Duck with Turnips

The meat content of a whole duck is low, which is why breasts (*magrets*) are so popular, while legs are an economical way to produce a delicious meal. Many different varieties of duck are cooked in France. The renowned breeds are Barbary, which are raised in the wild and have a gentle musky flavour, Nantes (or Challens, named after the marshland area where the duck lives), which has a delicately flavoured flesh, and Rouen, the most well-known, which has an exceptionally fine flesh and a special flavour because it is killed in such a way (smothering) that the blood remains in the muscles.

Preparation: 20 minutes
Cooking: 1 hour 15 minutes

Serves 6

1 tbsp olive oil
6 duck legs
sea salt
freshly ground black pepper
6 shallots, peeled
12 baby turnips, trimmed
1 large cooking apple, peeled, cored and chopped
20g flour
300ml cider
100ml vegetable stock

Heat the oven to 200°C/gas 6.

Place the olive oil in a large, heavy-based roasting tin and heat in the oven for 5 minutes. Stab the duck legs all over with a fork, rub with seasoning, then place in the roasting tin and cook for 20 minutes. Turn the duck legs, and add the whole shallots and turnips to the roasting tin. Baste with the fat, reduce the heat to 180°C/gas 4 and roast for a further 20 minutes.

Turn the duck legs again, and add the apple, moving the roasting vegetables to ensure they cook evenly. Roast for a further 20 minutes or until the duck is golden and crunchy and the vegetables soft and browned.

Remove the duck and vegetables from the roasting tin and place them on a warm serving dish. Drain off excess fat (reserve it for roasting or sautéing potatoes) and add the flour to the tin, mixing it in vigorously to make a roux. Then slowly add the cider and vegetable stock, stirring well to mix in the roasting flavours in the pan. Place directly over a medium heat and bring to a simmer, constantly stirring. Check the seasoning, pour over the duck and the roasted vegetables, and serve.

Duck Breasts in Orange

Magrets de Canard à l'Orange is a variation on the classic dish of duck with orange. Duck works well with sweet tastes, and this is a quick and stress-free version to prepare.

Preparation: 20 minutes
Cooking: 25 minutes

Serves 6

6 duck breasts with skin
20g butter
3 oranges
100ml fresh orange juice
1 tbsp vinegar
1 tbsp unrefined caster sugar
1 tbsp cornflour
2 tbsp Grand Marnier

Score the skin of each duck breast in a criss-cross pattern. Melt the butter in a large frying pan and cook the duck breasts, skin-side down, over a medium heat for 10 minutes, until the skin is golden and the fat has run out of it.

Meanwhile, use a sharp knife to peel the oranges down to the flesh, cutting away all the pith (do this over a plate to catch any escaping juice), and then cut into segments between the fine skin. Remove any pips.

Pour the fat away from the pan the duck breasts are cooking in, then cook the breasts, flesh-side down this time but still over a medium heat, for a further 8 minutes. Remove the meat from the pan and slice it, arrange it on a warm plate, top with the orange segments and keep it warm.

Add the orange juice to the pan (including any juice from the plate), along with the vinegar and sugar, and bring to a simmer. Remove from the heat. Mix the cornflour with a little water, add it to the pan and stir well until smooth. Finally pour in the Grand Marnier.

Pour the sauce over the sliced duck breasts and serve.

Fresh Foie Gras with Roasted Peaches

Foie gras has raised temperatures one way or another since Roman times. Horace's early writings describe a method of preparing geese that have been force-fed on figs. In the eleventh century Sainte Radegonde – one of France's many culinary saints – had a dish of *foie gras* prepared for the soon-to be-canonized Bishop of Poitiers, who thanked her with poems and odes in her honour. The marquis of Contades received a large fiefdom in Picardy from Louis XV as thanks for a gift of foie gras prepared by his pastry chef. Today it has become at the same time one of the most sought-after and one of the most vilified foodstuffs in the world, appreciated by gourmets for its incomparable texture and taste, and denounced for the method of its production. It is, however, one of the oldest and most fabled ingredients of the French kitchen, and I'd hate to see political correctness send it into culinary extinction, the way of peacock hearts and larks' tongues in aspic …

Preparation: 10 minutes, plus overnight marinating
Cooking: 25 minutes

Serves 6

1 fresh goose *foie gras* of about 800g
sea salt
freshly ground black pepper
50ml Madeira
50ml cognac
260g butter
5 fresh peaches, each destoned and cut into
8 wedges
a grating of nutmeg

Clean and trim the *foie gras* of any fibres or veins using a thin, sharp-bladed knife. Put it in a dish, add seasoning, Madeira and cognac, cover and marinate in the fridge overnight, turning it when you can in the evening before and the morning after.

The next day, remove the *foie gras* from the marinade and dry well with kitchen paper. Keep the marinade. Slice the *foie gras* into escalopes, each of about 100g.

Heat 100g of the butter in a large frying pan and, over high heat, sear the *foie gras* on each side for 45 seconds – or more if you must. Remove from the pan and keep warm. Add more butter if required and cook the peaches for 2 minutes, still over a high heat. Arrange the peaches on warmed plates and set aside.

Pour the marinade juices into the frying pan, bring to a simmer, then reduce the heat. Cut the remaining butter into small pieces and add it to the pan, whisking vigorously with a balloon whisk, until a glossy sauce is made. Add the nutmeg.

Arrange the *foie gras* on top of the peaches, spoon over the sauce and serve at once.

I picked up this way of cooking fresh *foie gras* – *Foie Gras Poëlé aux Pêches* – in the Gers, at the home of Madame Consularo, who runs the Château Bellevue in Cazaubon, near Eauze, and does all the cooking herself. She prepared this dish specially for me, and I've never had better.

MUSÉE

To flambé is simply to pour spirit over food and ignite it. The flaming dish creates a sensation, but, more than just a show, flambéing wonderfully enhances flavour too. The easiest way is to heat the spirit in a small saucepan, carefully ignite it and then pour the flaming liquid over the dish.

Quails with Cherries

Cailles Flambées is a simple but spectacular dish for a festive meal.

Preparation: 35 minutes
Cooking: 40 minutes

Serves 6

750g sour cherries, pitted
150ml red wine
a pinch of cinnamon
6 quails (your butcher will prepare them for you)
sea salt
freshly ground black pepper
25g butter
1 tbsp cornflour
50ml kirsch
50ml cognac

Take a generous third of the cherries, about 300g, and press them through a sieve to extract the juice. Or whiz the cherries in a blender and then pass them through a fine sieve – this is far quicker. Then put the juice, the remaining whole cherries, the red wine and cinnamon in a small saucepan, bring to the boil and simmer gently for 30 minutes.

Meanwhile, take the quails and season them on the inside. Melt the butter in a large pan, add the quails and cook them for 20 minutes until browned all over.

Add the cherry mix and juice to the quails, cover them and simmer for another 15 minutes, turning the quails halfway through cooking.

Remove the quails from the sauce and place on a warmed serving dish. Use a slotted spoon to remove the cherries, and scatter them over the quails. Set aside a spoonful of the liquid to cool. Then increase the heat under the remaining sauce to reduce it. Mix the cornflour with the cooled liquid, remove the sauce from the heat and quickly stir in the cornflour until smooth and blended. Return the sauce to the heat, stirring constantly until it thickens.

Pour the sauce over the quails, then heat and ignite the kirsch and cognac to flambé the dish just before serving (see the facing page).

Pigeon meat is tender and only slightly gamey, and the peas give it a succulent sweetness. Use young pigeons for this delicious dish, or try poussins for another version of it.

Pigeon with Peas

Ideally, you should use 4–5 month old pigeons and freshly shelled, small peas for this traditional recipe, *Pigeon aux Petits Pois*. For the bouquet garni, tie together a bundle of fresh herbs. I use sprigs of parsley, thyme, sage and rosemary, 2 bay leaves and a 5cm piece of leek.

Preparation: 15 minutes
Cooking: 30 minutes

Serves 6

70g butter
100g thick-cut bacon, cut into strips
8 shallots, finely diced
3 pigeons, cut in half (ask the butcher to do this)
100ml white wine
1 litre chicken stock
1 bouquet garni
sea salt
freshly ground black pepper
1kg freshly shelled peas
10g unrefined brown sugar
1 soft lettuce, such as Batavia or butterhead (Webbs), finely sliced
5 spring onions, finely sliced
a bunch of mint, finely chopped

Melt the butter in a large saucepan, add the bacon and shallots and cook until just golden, then remove from the pan with a slotted spoon. Add the pigeons and lightly brown all over on the outside. Add the white wine, stock, bouquet garni and seasoning, then return the cooked bacon and shallots and bring to the boil. Simmer for 15 minutes.

Add the peas, sugar and lettuce, stir well and simmer for a further 15 minutes, turning the pigeons so that they cook evenly.

Add the spring onions for the final 2 minutes of cooking. Serve garnished with freshly chopped mint leaves.

Christmas Turkey with Chestnuts

The traditional French Christmas meal takes place on Christmas Eve, and lasts long into the night. It's more usual to make this dish with goose, but you can use turkey – *Dinde aux Marrons* – as long as you ensure the meat doesn't dry out. For me, chestnuts have always evoked the spirit of the season, and in France they are often used as a main vegetable rather than simply a garnish. They have a sweetness that works very well with roasted meat, and, fortunately, using the tinned ones is just as good as buying them fresh. As for the turkey, to get one with its giblets you need to go to a good butcher who buys from small producers. Whether you can get a turkey with its giblets will tell you a great deal about the quality of your butcher.

Preparation: 20 minutes
Turkey cooking time: 20 minutes per 500g

Serves 8 to 10

For the stuffing:
2 x 450g packets or tins peeled chestnuts
500g sausagemeat
4 shallots, finely diced
2 cloves of garlic, crushed, peeled and chopped
a bunch of flat-leaf parsley, chopped
a bunch of sage, chopped
sea salt
freshly ground black pepper
1 egg

For the turkey:
1 x 4kg turkey with its giblets (if possible)
100g butter
6 sticks of celery, halved
6 carrots, peeled
6 red onions, peeled
100ml white wine
1 litre chicken or turkey stock
25g flour

Heat the oven to 180°C/gas 4.

To make the stuffing, slice half the chestnuts finely and place them in a bowl with the sausagemeat, shallots, garlic, parsley, sage, seasoning and egg. Mix well – this is best done using your hands.

Remove the giblets from the turkey and place to one side, then season the inside of the turkey and stuff with the freshly made mixture. Generously smear the outside of the turkey with butter.

Grease a heavy-based, deep roasting tin with a little of the remaining butter and add the giblets, celery and the whole carrots and onions. Pour over half the wine and half the chicken stock, and place the turkey on top. Cover generously with tin foil and cook in the middle of the oven for 1½ hours.

Remove the turkey from the oven and reduce the heat to 150°C/gas 2. Add the whole chestnuts and the remaining wine and stock, smear the turkey again with what remains of the butter, re-cover and return to the oven for a further 1–1½ hours. For the final 10 minutes of cooking, remove the tin foil and increase the heat to 180°C/gas 4 to give the turkey a golden skin. Remove from the oven, lift the turkey onto a carving plate and leave to rest in a warm place for 10–15 minutes – this allows the meat to relax and become more tender.

Discard the giblets. Carefully lift out the vegetables and chestnuts from the roasting tin and keep warm. Place the roasting tin directly on the heat and, using a flour dredger, shake in about 1 tablespoon of flour. Whisk vigorously and bring to the boil to make a coating gravy – adjust with more liquid (stock or water) or a little more flour to get the right consistency. Pass through a fine sieve, then check the seasoning. Serve the turkey with the chestnuts and vegetables and sauce.

Meat

Most French families now rely on simple grilled or roasted meats, with little accompaniment other than a sauce made from the meat's own juices. However, many traditional dishes rely on sauces and long cooking times for their success. The following dishes are old favourites which have been slightly adapted to make them easier to make, but which still convey some of the many textures, smells and tastes of the traditional French kitchen.

The essential thing when buying meat is to ensure it is of excellent quality. I find that, as with poultry, free-range organic meat is greatly superior in taste to the pre-packed, mass-produced variety. Befriend a good organic butcher, who will be able to recommend cuts of meat to suit the recipe you are planning, and bear in mind that whatever your personal standpoint on eating meat (and be it on ethical, taste or health grounds), it is always beneficial to know that what you are eating has been treated with respect before it reaches your table.

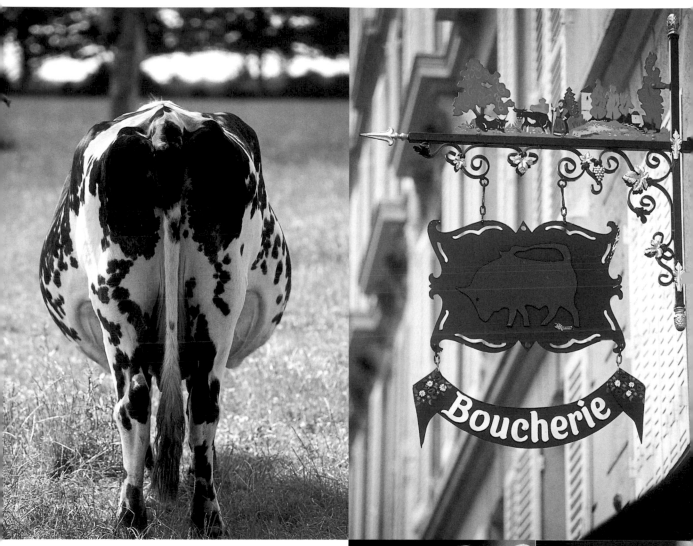

The French have a good tradition of local butchers who will advise and, if necessary, prepare your meat for you. Our local butcher used to come in a van and deliver the Sunday roast to us at my grandfather's house.

Paupiettes au Vin Blanc is one of my mother's recipes, which I associate with leisurely Sunday lunches in France with my grandparents. You can buy *paupiettes* ready-made in France, but they are quite easy to make at home – as our recipe demonstrates – and well worth the effort.

Veal Parcels in White Wine Sauce

The secret of this dish is in the cooking time: the longer you cook it, the better it gets, and if you make it the night before, the flavours will marry and intensify overnight, making a richer and tastier sauce.

Preparation: 40 minutes
Cooking: 1 hour 15 minutes

Serves 6

For the filling:
2 tbsp olive oil
100g mushrooms, chopped
1 red onion, diced
60g minced pork
2 cloves of garlic, crushed, peeled and chopped
a small bunch of flat-leaf parsley, chopped
a small bunch of sage, chopped
sea salt
freshly ground black pepper
30g breadcrumbs

For the veal:
6 thin veal escalopes
25g butter
3 red onions, peeled and cut in half
25g flour
500ml white wine
6 small carrots, peeled
600g new potatoes, peeled

Heat the oven to 180°C/gas 4.

Make the filling for the veal parcels: heat the olive oil in a frying pan, and sauté the mushrooms and the diced onion for 5 minutes. Add the pork, garlic, parsley, sage and seasoning, mix well and cook for another 5 minutes. Then remove from the heat, mix in the breadcrumbs and leave to cool a little.

Lay out the veal escalopes on the work surface and divide the filling among them. Fold in the ends and then roll up each escalope, tying with string to make little parcels.

Heat the butter in a frying pan and fry the veal parcels together with the halved red onions until the veal is golden. Remove the onions and veal and place in a casserole dish.

Add the flour to the pan where the escalopes were fried and stir it in well, gathering all the tasty bits into the mix. Then slowly add the white wine, stirring well, and bring to the boil. Take the sauce off the heat, pass it through a sieve, and pour it over the veal and onions.

Put the casserole in the oven and cook for 20 minutes. Take the casserole out, put in the carrots and potatoes, cover with a lid, and cook for a further 55 minutes. Serve hot.

Lentil and Toulouse Sausage Casserole

This casserole, *Lentilles–Saucisses à l'Ancienne*, is another old favourite: easy to make, completely stress-free and very versatile. It's great with country bread and strong red wine if you want a hot meal in a hurry. Toulouse sausages are made with pure pork and a generous amount of garlic. They vary from shop to shop according to personal recipes, so keep trying until you find your perfect one, or, if you prefer, use any other favourite sausage.

Preparation: 20 minutes, plus overnight soaking
Cooking: 40 minutes

Serves 6

300g green or brown lentils
2 tbsp olive oil
2 onions, diced
3 sticks of celery, chopped
2 cloves of garlic, crushed, peeled and chopped
3 sprigs of thyme
1 bay leaf
3 large tomatoes, peeled and chopped
2 tsp tomato purée
200ml red wine
400ml water, approximately
6 Toulouse or other favourite sausages, weighing about 750g in total
a large bunch of flat-leaf parsley

Soak the lentils overnight in water, then drain them and set them aside.

Heat the oven to 200°C/gas 6.

Heat the olive oil in a casserole dish, add the onion, celery and garlic and sauté for 5 minutes. Add the thyme leaves (stripped from the stalks), bay leaf, tomatoes and purée, mix together and cook for 5 minutes. Remove from the heat, add the lentils and red wine, stir well, then pour in enough water to cover. Place the sausages on top, cover with a lid and cook in the oven for 30 minutes. Stir in the parsley just before serving.

LE ST.VINCENT

SANDWICHERIE

Smoked Ham Winter Pot

Potée Auvergnate is a traditional French country dish. Every region has its variants, depending on the available vegetables, but this one is southern in character, thickened with chunky haricot beans and potatoes, perfect with a bottle of characterful red wine and an open fire …

Preparation: 40 minutes, plus overnight soaking
Cooking: 2 hours 15 minutes

Serves 6

500g haricot beans
1.5kg piece of smoked ham
6 small red onions, peeled
2 cloves of garlic, crushed, peeled and chopped
1 bay leaf
a sprig of thyme
freshly ground black pepper
1 tbsp Dijon mustard
6 carrots, cut into 5cm pieces
500g small to medium waxy potatoes, peeled but left whole
3 leeks, cut into 5cm pieces
sea salt
200g green beans, topped and tailed
a large bunch of flat-leaf parsley, finely chopped

Soak the haricot beans overnight in water. The next day drain and rinse them well.

Place the ham in a large casserole pot, cover with water and bring to a simmer, then cook for 10 minutes before draining and discarding the water. Return the ham to the casserole along with the onions, garlic, haricot beans, bay leaf, thyme, pepper and Dijon mustard. Just cover with water, gently bring up to the boil, skim off any residue and simmer for 1 1/2 hours with the lid on.

After the hour and a half has elapsed, add the carrots, potatoes and leeks to the casserole, cover and simmer for another 15 minutes.

Check the seasoning – you may not need to add salt. Add the green beans and parsley and cook for a further 5 minutes.

Lift out the ham, allow all the stock to run back into the casserole, and place the ham on a large carving board or plate. Slice the ham and serve it with the vegetables and cooking stock.

Pork with Blackcurrant

Porc au Cassis is easy to make, and the result is a wonderfully intense concentration of autumn flavours.

Preparation: 25 minutes
Cooking: 30 minutes

Serves 6

400g blackcurrants (frozen if out of season)
2 tbsp unrefined sugar
50ml water
1 tbsp olive oil
2 pork fillets, about 875g together, trimmed of fat
sea salt
freshly ground black pepper
60g butter
2 large cooking apples, peeled, cored and sliced
a pinch of cinnamon
1 tsp blackcurrant jam

Wash fresh blackcurrants, remove any stems, and place the fruit (fresh or frozen) in a small saucepan with the sugar and water. Cover and gently bring to boiling point, then remove from the heat. When they have cooled a little, drain the blackcurrants, reserving the juice. Set the juice and the blackcurrants aside.

Heat the oil in a sauté pan and fry the pork fillets over a medium heat until golden all over. Season, then cover and cook for another 15 minutes. When cooked, remove them from the pan and allow them to rest.

Meanwhile, heat 10g of the butter in a saucepan and fry the apples gently for 10 minutes or until golden. Add the cinnamon.

Put the reserved blackcurrant juice and the jam in the pan the pork was cooked in, bring to the boil and simmer. Cut the remaining butter into pieces and whisk it in, simmering rapidly, until a glossy sauce is made. Add the blackcurrants.

Slice the pork fillets and serve on a bed of the sautéed apples, topped with the blackcurrant sauce.

The sharpness of the blackcurrants cuts through the richness of the pork in this dish. It works well on its own, as above, or with steamed potatoes, which do not interfere with the balance of the dish.

Pork with Lentils

This simple dish, *Porc aux Lentilles*, combines Puy lentils and mustard to make a rich, creamy sauce. Puy lentils are grown only in the Velay region of France, and are famous for their green marbled appearance and excellent flavour. Here they carry the delicious sauce that goes so well with pork.

Preparation: 30 minutes
Cooking: 35 minutes

Serves 6

2 pork fillets, about 875g together, trimmed of fat
a bunch of sage
2 cloves of garlic, peeled and cut into slivers
1 lemon, from which small pieces of rind are cut
sea salt
freshly ground black pepper
1 tbsp olive oil
8 slices smoked streaky bacon, rind removed
1 litre chicken stock
250g Puy lentils
100ml white wine
100ml double cream or crème fraiche
1 tbsp Dijon mustard

Heat the oven to 180°C/gas 4.

Make slits in the pork with a small sharp knife and insert sage leaves, garlic slivers and pieces of lemon rind, then rub with seasoning.

Oil a baking tray with olive oil. Wrap the bacon around the pork. Place the bacon-wrapped fillets on the tray and cook for 35 minutes.

Put the chicken stock and lentils in a large saucepan and simmer gently for 30 minutes until the stock is absorbed. In another pan, combine the white wine, cream, mustard and seasoning and heat through gently. Slice the pork and serve with the lentils and mustard sauce.

Pork Chops with Mustard

Côtelettes de Porc à la Moutarde: a quick and easy way to make simple pork chops special. Good with Sauté Potates (page 167). For a real treat, include kidneys with pork chops.

Preparation: 15 minutes
Cooking: 35 minutes

Serves 6

6 pork chops
sea salt
100g butter
3 onions, finely diced
100ml white wine
2 tbsp Dijon mustard
100g small gherkins, sliced

Sprinkle the chops with salt. Melt 30g butter in a large frying pan, add the chops and cook for 12 minutes a side until golden brown all over.

Remove the pork chops from the pan and keep them warm. Add the onions to the pan and sauté over a gentle heat – do not frizzle or brown them. Pour in the white wine, increase the heat and reduce the sauce by half.

Mix in the mustard, reduce the heat again, then add the remaining butter in small pieces. Use a balloon whisk to form a smooth glossy sauce. Finally, stir in the gherkins and serve the sauce with the pork chops.

Roast Pork with Figs

For a perfect crunchy crackling, ask your butcher to score the pork skin in a close criss-cross pattern.

Preparation: 30 minutes
Cooking: 2 hours

Serves 6

2 tbsp olive oil
1¹/₂ kg boned and rolled loin of pork, skin well scored
fine sea salt
freshly ground black pepper
20 ripe figs
200ml white wine
100ml water
20g flour
100ml vegetable water

Heat the oven to 200°C/gas 6.

Put the olive oil in a large, heavy-based roasting tin and heat it in the oven. Rub the scored pork with salt and pepper. Take the tin out of the oven, put in the pork and roll it in the hot oil to cover it evenly. Return the tin to the oven and cook the pork for 40 minutes, then reduce the temperature to 180°C/gas 4 and cook it for a further 40 minutes. At this point, return the oven to its original temperature of 200°C/gas 6: this will help to get that final crunch on the crackling.

Take the tin out of the oven, prick the figs all over with a fork and place them around the roasting pork, add half the white wine and all of the water, and return the tin to the hot oven. After 15 minutes, remove it from the oven and baste the figs with the cooking juices, then return and cook for a further 10 minutes.

Remove from the oven. Transfer the pork to a warm carving board or plate and allow it to rest for 10 minutes in a warm place. Remove the figs and keep them warm.

Make a sauce with the cooking juices from the figs and pork: sprinkle the flour into the roasting tin and stir it well to absorb the oils and juices. Over a low to medium heat, gradually add the remaining white wine and the vegetable water to the paste, mixing well. Allow to simmer and thicken. Check the seasoning, adjust the consistency if necessary with extra water and pass through a sieve.

Carve the pork and serve it with the figs. Serve the sauce separately or poured over the figs.

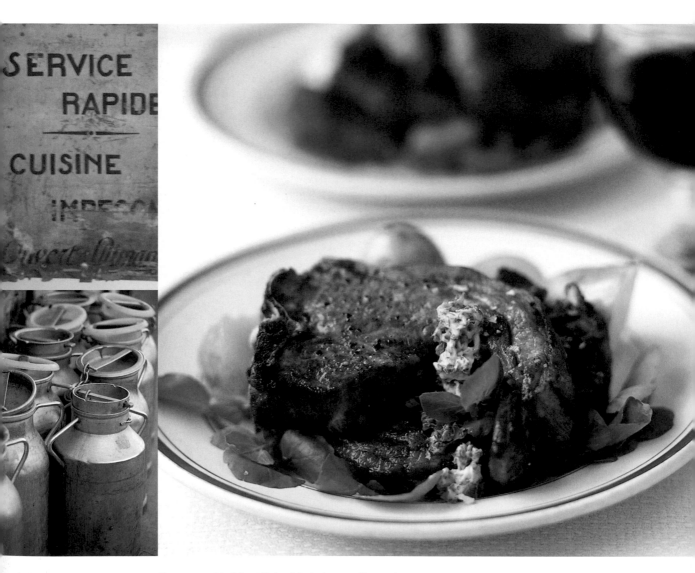

If you travel to Mont Saint-Michel, you will see the lambs grazing on the very green marshland by the water's edge, or even nibbling on the seaweed growing on the rocks.

Lamb Chops Vert Pré

The crisp, fresh watercress is an excellent accompaniment to tender lamb and new potatoes (Jersey Royals are terrific with this). Traditionally, the lambs are fed on the grass of reclaimed land by the sea, and have a delicate, slightly salty taste, hence the name: *Côtelettes d'Agneau Vert Pré*. A perfect dish for springtime.

Preparation: 15 minutes
Cooking: 30 minutes

Serves 6

500g new potatoes, washed
12 lamb chops
sea salt
freshly ground black pepper
100g butter, softened
a bunch of curly parsley, finely chopped
juice of 1/2 lemon
200g watercress, trimmed

Simmer the new potatoes for 20 minutes or until cooked.

Set the grill to hot. Arrange the chops in the grill pan, sprinkle with seasoning and cook under the hot grill: 6 minutes each side for rare, 8 minutes for medium and 10 minutes for well done.

Cut the butter into knobs, place in a bowl with the finely chopped parsley, lemon juice and seasoning, and mix well.

Arrange the potatoes and watercress on plates, top with the lamb chops and scoops of the butter, and serve.

Lamb Navarin

This dish would originally have been made with mutton, which would have needed a longer cooking time, but this version, *Navarin d'Agneau,* uses lamb for a sweet and tender casserole.

Preparation: 30 minutes
Cooking: 1 hour 40 minutes

Serves 6

2 kg boneless leg or shoulder of lamb, cubed
3 tbsp flour
3 tbsp olive oil
1 litre vegetable stock
2 cloves of garlic, crushed and peeled
6 shallots, peeled and left whole
2 x 410g cans chopped tomatoes or 800g fresh tomatoes, peeled
1 tbsp tomato purée
150ml red wine
2 bay leaves
2 sprigs of marjoram
1/2 tsp smoked sweet paprika
sea salt
freshly ground black pepper
200g small carrots
200g small turnips
300g new potatoes

Trim the lamb of any fat. Place in a bowl with the flour and toss to coat the cubes of meat evenly. Heat the olive oil in a large casserole dish, add just enough meat to cover the bottom of the pan and brown the meat all over. Remove and repeat with the next batch, until all the meat is browned. Return all the meat to the pan, add the stock, and bring to a simmer, mixing well. Add the garlic, shallots, chopped tomatoes, purée, red wine, bay leaves, marjoram, paprika and seasoning. Bring to boiling point and simmer gently for 1 hour, stirring from time to time.

Add the whole, prepared carrots, turnips and potatoes to the casserole, making sure they are covered in liquid. You may need to add a little more stock or water at this point. Cook for a further 20 minutes or until the vegetables are soft, then serve.

Braised Lamb Shanks

The dish has to be cooked slowly and gently for maximum flavour and tenderness. Serve with mashed potato.

Preparation: 20 minutes, plus marinating overnight
Cooking: 2 hours 10 minutes

Serves 6

For the marinade:
4 cloves of garlic, crushed and peeled
1 tbsp dried juniper berries
zest of 1 lemon
10 shallots, peeled and left whole
1 sprig of rosemary
350ml red wine
sea salt
freshly ground black pepper

For the lamb:
6 lamb shanks
3 tbsp olive oil
10 plum tomatoes, peeled
40g flour
120ml red wine
a bunch of flat-leaf parsley, chopped

Prepare the marinade: put the garlic, juniper berries, lemon zest, shallots, rosemary and red wine in a large, shallow dish. Add seasoning, then put in the lamb shanks and turn them to coat them well. Leave to marinate overnight.

The next day, heat the oven to 180°C/gas 4.

Lightly oil a heavy-based roasting tray. Transfer the lamb shanks and marinade to the tray, cover and cook for 1 hour. Remove from the oven, turn the shanks and add the plum tomatoes. Return to the oven and cook for a further hour, until the meat is soft and tender.

When ready to serve, remove the shanks from the pan and keep them warm while you make the sauce. Put the roasting tray over a low heat, sprinkle in the flour and blend it with all the cooking juices. Gradually whisk in the red wine, bring to the boil, then stir in the parsley. Pour over the lamb shanks and tomatoes and serve.

White Pudding with Truffled Pasta

In France white pudding is often given to children, and it remains one of the great memory dishes of my childhood, simply grilled or fried and eaten with buttered pasta. This rather more grown-up version – *Boudin Blanc aux Tagliatelles Truffées* – uses white truffle, which gives it a sophisticated, earthy flavour.

Preparation: 10 minutes
Cooking: 20 minutes

Serves 6

6 white puddings
600g fresh ribbon pasta
2 tbsp truffle oil
sea salt
freshly ground black pepper
1 white truffle

Heat the grill to medium.

Place the white puddings on the grill pan and cook for 12 minutes or until golden brown, turning occasionally.

Meanwhile, bring a large pan of water to the boil, add the pasta and cook according to packet or shop instructions. Drain and shake the colander to remove every last drop of water.

Warm a large serving dish. Pour half of the truffle oil and a little seasoning into the dish and turn to coat the inside. Add the pasta, drizzle over the remaining oil and sprinkle with a little more seasoning. Toss well.

Slice the white pudding. Finely slice the white truffle using a truffle slicer. Add both to the pasta and serve at once.

Black Pudding and Apple

A classic Breton combination, *Boudin aux Pommes* is terrific with buckwheat pancakes (page 49) or sautéed potatoes, and a crisp green side salad. *Boudin noir*, French black pudding, is very simply made from seasoned pig's blood and fat, with regional additions that can vary from cooked onions to grated raw onions or even apples, prunes or chestnuts.

Preparation: 20 minutes
Cooking: 15 minutes

Serves 6

olive oil for frying
6 black puddings, cut into 2.5cm slices
3 thick rashers bacon, chopped
25g butter
5 Bramley apples, peeled, cored and cut into wedges
pinch of freshly grated nutmeg
sea salt
freshly ground black pepper

Heat a drizzle of oil in a large frying pan, add the black pudding and bacon and cook over a medium-high heat for 2 minutes on each side. Then reduce the heat to low.

While the black pudding and bacon cook, melt the butter in another frying pan, add the apple and nutmeg, mix, and cook on a high heat for about 4 minutes or until the apple colours and just softens.

Add the apple to the black pudding and bacon, season and cook for 5 more minutes over the low heat, then serve.

White pudding – *boudin blanc* – is a little harder to find in Britain than in France (although it's easy to get hold of in Ireland), but it is worth pestering your butcher for. It's white sausage, particularly associated with Christmas, and made from finely ground poultry, veal, pork or rabbit, mixed with spices and cream.

Fillet Steak with Tarragon

This simple but effective way of preparing steaks dates back to the seventeenth century. Use lots of fresh tarragon for a sharp and delicious contrast with the creamy sauce. Try to buy French tarragon: it has a fine, aniseed-like flavour.

Preparation: 10 minutes
Cooking: 10 minutes

Serves 6

25g butter
6 open flat mushrooms
olive oil for frying
4 shallots, diced
100ml white wine
50ml double cream
1 tbsp grainy mustard (such as Meaux)
1 clove of garlic, crushed, peeled and chopped
a bunch of French tarragon, chopped
sea salt
freshly ground black pepper
6 x 150g fillet steaks

Melt the butter in a frying pan over a medium heat and cook the mushrooms on both sides until golden. Reduce the heat and keep warm until needed.

Heat a little olive oil in a saucepan over a medium heat and fry the shallots until soft and golden. Add the wine and simmer for 3 minutes, then reduce the heat and add the cream, mustard, garlic, tarragon and seasoning, and gently warm through. Do not allow to boil.

Heat a drizzle of olive oil in a large frying pan over a high heat and fry the steaks: 1½ minutes each side for rare, 2½ minutes each side for medium and 3 minutes each side for well done (if you must!).

Serve the steaks on the cooked mushrooms topped with the sauce.

This dish must have been a blessing for seventeenth-century chefs. It takes scarcely any time to cook, but is sophisticated enough to please the most exacting nobleman.

Boeuf en Daube

This is the most traditional of the inland Provençal dishes. According to the old story, it was invented by a farmer's wife, who, having put a piece of beef in the oven to cook, began gossiping with a friend, lost track of time, and found the pot dry and the meat burnt. In an attempt to save dinner, she added more water into the pot, but forgot it again and it burnt a second time. Desperate to hide her mistake, the farmer's wife added herbs, wine and vegetables to the pot, so that by the end of the day the resulting dish was so sweet and tender that all her neighbours wanted the recipe. The secret is in the cooking time. My great-grandmother used to cook it in an earthenware pot at a very low heat for three days, but this version has been reduced to a more manageable three and a half hours. Serve with new season boiled potatoes or noodles tossed in a little butter.

Preparation: 30 minutes, plus overnight marinating
Cooking: 3 1/2 hours

Serves 6

For the casserole:
1.75kg piece of rump steak
4 tbsp olive oil
2 onions, sliced
2 cloves of garlic, crushed, peeled and chopped
3 tbsp flour, plus more for dusting
1 tbsp drained capers
100g black olives
1 x 410g tin chopped tomatoes
zest of 1 orange
200g carrots, chopped into 5cm pieces
125g small brown mushrooms
a bunch of flat-leaf parsley

For the marinade:
1 bottle white wine
2 bay leaves
sea salt
freshly ground black pepper

Combine the marinade ingredients in a large bowl, add the rump steak and cover. Leave to marinate overnight, turning from time to time in the evening and during the following day.

Remove the beef from the marinade and pat it dry with kitchen paper. Retain the marinade.

Heat 2 tablespoons of the olive oil in a casserole pan over a low-medium heat. Add the onions and garlic and sauté gently for 8 minutes. Sprinkle in the flour and mix well, then pour in the marinade a little at a time, stirring constantly. When all the liquid has been stirred in, add the capers, olives, tomatoes and orange zest, and allow to simmer.

Heat the oven to 140°C/gas 1.

Heat the remaining olive oil in a frying pan over a high heat. Dust the rump of beef in flour and add it to the hot oil. Brown all over to seal.

Transfer the beef to the casserole and ladle some of the juice back to the frying pan to lift off the delicious meaty bits from the side of the pan. Return the juice to the casserole. Bring the casserole to a simmer, cover with a lid, place in the oven and cook for 2 hours.

When the 2 hours are up, add the carrots and mushrooms and then cook for a further hour.

To serve, lift the beef out on to a carving plate and carve it into thickish slices. Stir the parsley into the vegetables and juices, check the seasoning and spoon it over the slices of beef.

Rabbit with Chestnut Purée

Rabbit has always been a staple in France, and although in England it has been out of favour for many years, it has finally begun to make a comeback. This recipe – *Lapin à la Purée de Marrons* – makes the most of the rich, dark flesh of the rabbit and the sweet flouriness of the chestnuts. This is a perfect dish for autumn.

Preparation: 15 minutes
Cooking: 1 hour

Serves 6

1 rabbit, cut into 6 joints (ask your butcher)
sea salt
freshly ground black pepper
80g butter
150g thick-cut bacon, finely chopped
1 tin puréed chestnuts (unsweetened)
300ml chicken stock
200ml white wine
200g watercress

Heat the oven to 180°C/gas 4.

Take the rabbit joints and season them. Melt the butter in a large casserole, add the rabbit along with the bacon, and toss to coat with the butter. Cover and cook in the oven for 20 minutes, then turn the rabbit, return the lid and cook for a further 20 minutes.

Remove the rabbit and set it aside in a warm place. Add the chestnut purée, stock and wine to the casserole dish, place it over a medium heat and bring it to the boil. Use a balloon whisk to work the purée into the mix, making a rich sauce.

Serve the roasted rabbit with the chestnut sauce on a bed of watercress.

Rabbit with Red Rice

A warming country dish, in which the red rice absorbs and enriches the flavours of wine and rabbit.

Preparation: 20 minutes
Cooking: 1 hour 45 minutes

Serves 6

2 tbsp olive oil
1 rabbit, cut into 6 joints (ask your butcher)
1 red onion, diced
2 sprigs of thyme
1 bay leaf
225g red rice
1 whole garlic bulb, cut in half crossways and roasted (see page 40)
500g plum tomatoes, peeled, quartered and deseeded
100ml white wine
sea salt
freshly ground black pepper

Heat the oven to 150°C/gas 2.

Heat the olive oil in a large casserole over a medium heat. Add the rabbit joints, brown all over – about 10 minutes – then remove. Add the onion, thyme sprigs and bay leaf to the casserole and sauté for 2 minutes. Add the red rice, stirring well to coat the grains in oil and juices, then return the rabbit. Ease the garlic flesh out of its skin and stir it into the casserole with the tomatoes, wine and seasoning. Add water so that the rice is covered with liquid. Mix well, bring to the boil and reduce the heat to very low. Put the lid on and cook for 30 minutes. Stir from time to time and check that the rice does not stick to the bottom of the pan: add a little more wine, or water, if the rice threatens to stick. Serve at once.

Red rice, grown in the Camargue region of France, is nuttier in flavour than ordinary arborio rice, but does not demand as much cooking time as brown rice. It gives a lovely rich colour to this autumn dish.

Vegetables

Traditionally, French dishes were not served with vegetables unless these were an integral part of the dish (such as *Pigeon aux Petits Pois*, *Dinde aux Marrons*). Vegetable dishes would be served as a separate course, although nowadays this is not as common as it once was. As a result, there are many traditional French vegetable-based dishes that can very easily be adapted as main courses for people who prefer not to eat meat or fish.

Living as I do with two strict vegetarians, I find that vegetable dishes play a much greater part in my life than they did in my mother's. It's very hard to be vegetarian in France – although the markets are filled with the most fabulous produce – because to most French people the ethos of vegetarianism is incomprehensible and foreign (my mother still looks at Anouchka with suspicion, and asks her if she is eating properly, although you've never seen such a disgustingly healthy child).

I am quite happy to prepare and eat vegetarian food at home (although many non-vegetarian French dishes have too many personal and cultural associations for me ever to forsake them completely). However, as with all the recipes in this book, the quality of the ingredients is the secret to the success of the dish. Locally grown produce in season is by far the best, and you should try to make the most of it whenever possible. There is little to beat the taste of freshly picked green peas, or buttered new potatoes, or fresh, tender green beans, or sun-warmed tomatoes drizzled with lemon juice and oil.

And as in so many things to do with food, the anticipation – waiting for the strawberries or the young sprouting broccoli to come into season; enjoying the autumn flavours of pumpkin or blackberries or squash – becomes a significant part of the pleasure …

ts Artisa

LE ROUGE GORGE

s d'Epices, Co

French markets are one of the great pleasures of
the summer. Stalls of brightly coloured fruit and
vegetables, spices, olives and mushrooms are as
much a delight to the eyes as to the palate, and in
the warmth of the morning sun, the scent is heavenly.

Anouchka's Pumpkin Seed Mushrooms

My daughter invented this recipe when she was three years old by accidentally dropping the contents of a box of pumpkin seeds into a dish I was preparing. The child shows promise … Serve with jacket potatoes, pasta or on toast with a green salad.

Preparation: 10 minutes
Cooking: 15 minutes

Serves 6

300g brown cap mushrooms
olive oil
25g butter
4 shallots, chopped
3 cloves of garlic, crushed, peeled and chopped
25g pumpkin seeds
sea salt
freshly ground black pepper
juice of 1/2 lemon
150ml white wine
2 tsp grainy mustard (such as Meaux)
3 tbsp double cream

Separate the stems and caps of the mushrooms. Finely chop the stems and slice the tops.

Heat a little oil with the butter in a large frying pan and cook the mushrooms over a medium heat, stirring constantly, until they are golden brown: about 8 minutes. Add the shallots, garlic and pumpkin seeds and cook for a further 4 minutes. Add the seasoning, lemon juice and wine, simmer for 4 minutes, then stir in the mustard and cream. Stir well, allow to simmer for 2 minutes, and then serve.

Imbach Mushrooms

When I was small we sometimes went hunting for mushrooms in the woods with our friends, the Imbachs. I don't remember actually finding any myself (except for once when I found a puffball the size of a beach-ball, and was very disappointed to be told we couldn't eat it), but that didn't stop me trying. This dish is great with any kind of mushrooms, although the larger ones do tend to have more flavour.

Preparation: 10 minutes, plus 1 hour's marinating
Cooking: 8 minutes

Serves 6

12 open, flat mushrooms, or other favourites
6 tbsp olive oil
3 cloves of garlic, crushed, peeled and chopped
200ml red wine
5 tbsp cognac
sea salt
freshly ground black pepper
large bunch of flat-leaf parsley, finely chopped
6 slices of baguette

Place the mushrooms, olive oil, garlic, wine, cognac and seasoning in a large bowl and toss well to coat evenly. Leave to marinate for 1 hour.

Heat the oven to 180°C/gas 4.

Put the mushrooms with their marinade on a roasting tray and cook for 6 minutes, then turn them over and cook for a further 4 minutes. Move the mushrooms around to ensure even cooking.

Sprinkle the parsley over the mushrooms and return to the oven for another 2 minutes.

Lightly toast the slices of baguette. Pile the mushrooms on to the warm bread and drizzle with any cooking juices.

This dish is perfect to make with autumn field mushrooms, and tastes so good that I can quite happily eat it as a main course with a green salad. Cep (porcini) mushrooms – *Boletus edulis* – also work very well prepared in this way, if you are lucky enough to find some, or you could try a mixture of wild and cultivated mushrooms.

Although this is, strictly speaking, an Italian dish, I couldn't resist including it here as it is one of the great comfort foods of winter. I like to make it with the local Noirmoutier potatoes, an ancient variety dating back to the sixteenth century, and perfect for this dish.

Spinach Gnocchi

This is a great cold-weather dish: rich, warm and flavoursome. Ideal for lazy nights in.

Preparation: 40 minutes
Cooking: 30 minutes

Serves 6

600g floury potatoes, peeled and cut into pieces
350g spinach, trimmed and washed
150g flour, plus extra for dusting
1 egg yolk
sea salt
freshly ground black pepper
75g butter
100g blue vein cheese
a bunch of basil

Place the potatoes in a saucepan of boiling water and simmer for 20 minutes. Drain, return to the pan over a low heat and, shaking the pan, allow the excess moisture to steam off. Mash the potatoes until smooth.

Cook the spinach in a large pan over a medium heat with no added moisture, mixing constantly until wilted and soft. When cooked, place in a clean kitchen cloth. Gather the corners together and twist tightly to squeeze out every last drop of moisture, then finely chop the spinach.

Place the mashed potatoes, spinach, flour, egg yolk and seasoning in a large bowl and mix until evenly blended and a soft pliable dough forms. Dust your hands and a board or tray with flour. Take small nuggets of the dough, roll it into balls and place them on the board. You should end up with about 60. Using a fork, gently flatten each ball, allowing the tines of the fork to make indentations across the top.

Heat a large pan of water just to boiling point then reduce the heat. To the simmering water add just enough gnocchi so that they have room to roam around, and cook for 2 minutes or until they rise to the surface. Remove and drain well, and cook the next batch.

Heat the oven to 180°C/gas 4. Lightly butter a large low-sided ovenproof dish.

Place a layer of the cooked gnocchi in the dish, then crumble in some of the blue cheese. Continue to layer the gnocchi and cheese, adding seasoning and the remaining butter cut up into little pieces as you go. Cook until golden and bubbling: about 10 minutes. Scatter torn basil leaves over the top and serve.

Gratin Dauphinois

The ultimate potato dish. It's so good that I'm quite happy to have this as a main course, although it also works very well as an accompaniment to meat, fish or green vegetables.

Preparation: 30 minutes
Cooking: 1 hour 45 minutes

Serves 6

1kg potatoes, such as King Edwards, Desirée, Idaho or Maris Piper
1 clove of garlic, crushed and peeled
100g butter
20fl oz single cream
sea salt
freshly ground black pepper
100g Gruyère cheese, grated

Heat the oven to 150°C/gas 2.

Peel the potatoes and slice them finely using a mandolin or a food processor. Place the potato slices in a large bowl of cold water and move them around to get rid of excess starch. Drain well and dry thoroughly: use a salad spinner or else put the slices in a tea towel, gather the corners together, go outside and swing your arm as fast and vigorously as you can …

Rub a large shallow ovenproof dish with the garlic clove and a little butter.

Put the remaining butter with the cream in a large saucepan and bring just to the boil. Finely dice what's left of the garlic and add it to the butter and cream, along with seasoning and the potato slices. Gently simmer for 8 minutes.

Transfer to the prepared dish, spread out evenly and top with the Gruyère and a little more seasoning. Bake for 1¹/₂ hours. Serve hot.

Gratin Dauphinois has everything you need in a main course: a creamy, satisfying texture, lots of flavour and a golden, crispy surface. The story I heard was that it was created for the *dauphin* – the young prince soon to become Henri II – to encourage him to eat his vegetables.

Gratin Dauphinois is well worth the preparation it takes. Slice the potatoes on a mandolin (you can buy these very reasonably), then rinse the slices in fresh water to get rid of starch. Dry them in a salad spinner or a tea towel. The rest is easy, but do not rush the cooking. The result is perfection.

Boulangère Potatoes

This dish takes time; don't rush it! The result is worth it: meltingly tender potato slivers topped with a crunchy, golden crust like French bread, hence the name, *Pommes Boulangère*.

Preparation: 25 minutes
Cooking: 90 minutes

Serves 6

1kg floury potatoes, such as Maris Piper, Desirée, King Edwards or Idaho
2 onions
25g butter
300ml hot chicken or vegetable stock
sea salt
freshly ground black pepper
a few sprigs of thyme

Heat the oven to 180°C/gas 4.

Peel the potatoes and slice them very finely using a mandolin or a food processor. Slice the onions in the same way.

Butter an ovenproof dish and make layers of the potatoes and onions, with seasoning and the thyme leaves (stripped from the stalks) sprinkled over each. Finish with a layer of potatoes and try to make a neat overlapping pattern with them. Using the flat of your hand, press down the potatoes firmly.

Pour in the hot stock. Cut the remaining butter into little pieces and dot the top with them. Cover with tin foil and cook for 1 hour.

Remove the foil and bake for a further 30 minutes. The potato should be soft all the way through and the top layer golden brown.

Nutmeg Mash

Proper mash is one of life's small but significant delights. Having tasted this, I just can't understand the packet stuff at all …

Preparation: 10 minutes
Cooking: 30 minutes

Serves 6

1.5kg floury potatoes, such as Maris Piper, Desirée, King Edwards or Idaho
175g butter
300ml milk
1 egg
1/4 tsp freshly grated nutmeg
sea salt
freshly ground black pepper

Peel the potatoes, cut into pieces, place in a saucepan of boiling water and simmer for 20 minutes. Drain well, return to the pan over a low heat and, shaking the pan, allow the excess moisture to steam off. Mash the potatoes until smooth – for perfect mash try using a hand-held ricer.

Place the butter and milk in a saucepan over a medium heat and gently bring to the boil. Slowly pour the melted butter and hot milk into the potatoes, mixing well with a rubber spatula. Break in the egg and beat. Finally, add the nutmeg and seasoning. Mix well, taste and adjust to your personal choice. Serve at once.

Sauté Potatoes

Pommes de Terre Sautées are an excellent accompaniment to roast meat or fish, although I think they are good enough to eat as a main course with a crunchy green salad.

Preparation: 10 minutes
Cooking: 30 minutes

Serves 6

2kg floury potatoes, such as Maris Piper, Desirée, King Edwards or Idaho
8 tbsp olive oil
sea salt
freshly ground black pepper

Peel the potatoes and cook whole in gently boiling water for 12 minutes. Drain and slice into 1cm rounds. Heat the oven to 180°C/gas 4.

Divide the oil between two big frying pans and heat. Place a layer of potatoes over the base of each pan and cook for 5 minutes on each side until golden.

Remove with a slotted spoon and place in a roasting tray with a crumpled up piece of baking parchment in the bottom (this prevents the potatoes on the bottom from going soggy). Keep warm in the hot oven. Repeat until all the potatoes are cooked.

Sprinkle with sea salt and black pepper, and serve at once.

Roasted Asparagus Spears

This is a simple and delicious way to prepare asparagus, and works wonderfully in salads.

Preparation: 10 minutes
Cooking: 10 minutes

Serves 6

500g green asparagus spears
3 tbsp olive oil
sea salt
freshly ground black pepper
juice of 1 lemon
a dash of balsamic vinegar
100g Parmesan cheese

Trim the white ends from the asparagus; I sometimes like to cut at an angle.

Heat the oven to 200°C/gas 6.

Drizzle a large non-stick baking tray with the olive oil, add the asparagus, toss them in the oil, then roast them for 10 minutes. The asparagus around the edge of the tray may be better roasted, so cook the middle pieces for a few minutes longer if needed.

Transfer the roasted asparagus to a serving dish and add seasoning, lemon juice and balsamic vinegar. With a vegetable peeler, carve ribbons of Parmesan over the top. Serve hot or at room temperature.

Snap up fresh green asparagus in season and prepare this wonderful – and wonderfully easy – dish. Eat the asparagus either soon after roasting, while still hot, or save to eat at room temperature later in the day: on a picnic, perhaps.

Green Beans with Pine Nuts

At my grandparents' house I remember throwing closed pinecones into the open fire to make the pine nuts pop out ready-toasted – this has the advantage of being alarming to adults and potentially hazardous, and is therefore tremendous fun. Nowadays you can buy pine nuts in packets at the supermarket, which is less fun, but much easier. These green beans are great served with roast lamb, or added to lightly cooked pasta with chopped tomato and a squeeze of lemon.

Preparation: 10 minutes
Cooking: 8 minutes

Serves 6

400g fine green beans, topped and tailed
50g pine nuts
25g butter
3 tbsp white wine

Plunge the beans into boiling water and cook for 2 minutes.

Heat a non-stick frying pan, and dry-fry the pine nuts – vigilantly – until golden brown. Take care: nothing seems to happen, then suddenly the pine nuts colour.

Drain the beans well and place in a pan with the butter and white wine. Cover and cook for a further minute, add the toasted pine nuts, toss and serve.

Courgettes with Lemon Butter

My grandfather used to grow giant (and quite inedible) marrows in his garden, living by the rule that the bigger they got, the better they were. These baby marrows, however, are at their most sweet and tender, and make an excellent accompaniment to fish or vegetable dishes.

Preparation: 10 minutes
Cooking: 10 minutes

Serves 6

40g butter
2 tbsp olive oil
6 medium courgettes
zest and juice of 1 lemon
sea salt
freshly ground black pepper

Place the butter and oil in a large frying pan and gently heat. Cut the courgettes at an angle into slices about 2.5cm thick. Increase the heat under the oil and melted butter and add a layer of the sliced courgettes, frying them on each side until golden. Remove and keep warm, and repeat until all the courgettes are cooked. Return the courgettes to the pan, add the lemon zest and juice and the seasoning, toss and serve at once.

Ratatouille can be as simple or as complicated as you want to make it. The main rule is that the longer you cook it, the better it becomes. So, as with all casseroles, make it a day in advance to allow the flavours to merge.

Ratatouille

For variations, try using red wine instead of water, or chillies for extra bite. This is very good with Anouchka's Chilli Garlic Bread (page 61).

Preparation: 30 minutes
Cooking: 1 hour 10 minutes

Serves 6

9 tbsp olive oil
2 red onions, chopped
2 cloves of garlic, crushed, peeled and chopped
3 red peppers, deseeded and roughly chopped
2 aubergines, roughly chopped
4 courgettes, roughly chopped
3 x 410g tins chopped tomatoes, or 1kg fresh tomatoes, skinned
400ml water
a bunch of oregano, chopped
a bunch of marjoram, chopped
a bunch of flat-leaf parsley, chopped
sea salt
freshly ground black pepper

Heat 3 tablespoons of the olive oil in a large saucepan over a medium heat, add the onions and garlic and sauté for 3 minutes. Add the peppers, aubergines and courgettes, mix well and cook for a further 5 minutes or until the vegetables have gained a little colour. Then add the tomatoes, water, herbs and seasoning, mix well and simmer gently over a reduced heat for a further hour, stirring from time to time. When cooked stir in another 6 tablespoons of olive oil and check the seasoning. Serve hot or at room temperature.

Spiced Red Cabbage

This wonderfully comforting dish for autumn and winter is filled with rich, sweet flavours. Best made a day ahead and reheated, it works very well with baked ham, duck or even roast chicken, although I am happy to eat it on its own.

Preparation: 30 minutes
Cooking: 1 hour 15 minutes

Serves 6

50g butter
1 tbsp olive oil
1 small red cabbage, finely sliced
1 red onion, finely sliced
1 red chilli, finely sliced (seeds included if you like the heat)
100ml red wine vinegar or 50ml balsamic
75g unrefined brown sugar
1/2 tsp allspice
1/2 tsp ground cloves
sea salt
freshly ground black pepper
200ml water

Melt the butter with the oil in a saucepan over a medium heat, add the red cabbage, onion and chilli, stir well and cook for 10 minutes. Add the vinegar, sugar, allspice, cloves, seasoning and water, mix well and bring to the boil. Reduce the heat, cover and simmer the dish for 1 hour, checking frequently. If the mixture becomes dry during cooking, add a little more water. Serve hot or reheated.

Roast Vegetables with Couscous

I'm a great fan of couscous, which I use with all kinds of ingredients as an alternative to rice or pasta. It's ridiculously quick and easy to make, healthy, delicious, and has the capacity to soak up flavours, making it extremely versatile. This is a vegetarian version, which can be enjoyed entirely on its own, or as an accompaniment to a meat or fish dish, or with a salad. Try it with a handful of raisins and chopped apricots, and plenty of chopped fresh mint.

Preparation: 30 minutes
Cooking: 40 minutes

Serves 6

4 tbsp olive oil, plus a little extra to serve
2 onions, peeled and cut into wedges
2 shallots, peeled
3 carrots, cut into chunks
2 parsnips, cut into chunks
3 cloves of garlic, crushed, peeled and chopped
1 red chilli, finely sliced (seeds included if you like the heat)
1 tsp paprika
1/2 tsp ground cinnamon
1/2 tsp coriander seeds, crushed
1/2 tsp cumin seeds, crushed
4 cardamom pods, crushed
large pinch of saffron
2 courgettes, thickly sliced
500g plum tomatoes, skinned
sea salt
freshly ground black pepper
450g couscous
75g butter
a bunch of flat-leaf parsley, chopped
a bunch of coriander, chopped
a dash of balsamic vinegar

Heat the oven to 190°C/gas 5.

Heat the olive oil in a large, heavy-based roasting tin directly over a medium heat. Add the onions, shallots, carrots and parsnips and cook for about 10 minutes until golden, stirring frequently. Add the garlic, chilli, paprika, cinnamon, coriander, cumin and cardamom and stir well, coating the vegetables in all the spices. Cook for a further 4 minutes then remove from the heat and stir in the saffron, courgettes, tomatoes and seasoning. Transfer to the oven to roast for 40 minutes. Check after 30 minutes, adding a little water or vegetable stock if desired.

Place the couscous in a large bowl and cover with boiling water to a level of 2.5cm above the grains. Mix well and leave to stand for 5 minutes. Meanwhile, melt the butter in a small saucepan, add the chopped herbs and cook for 1 minute. Pour over the couscous, mix well and season it.

Take the vegetables out of the oven, drizzle with olive oil and balsamic vinegar, and serve with the couscous.

My daughter loves making these crisp roasted peppers, and designing new fillings for them. Try them with rice, or couscous with dried fruit, or slices of pancetta – the variations are endless.

Baked Red Peppers

Use good, well-ripened red peppers for a
cheery, colourful summer dish.

Preparation: 25 minutes
Cooking: 1 hour 25 minutes

Serves 6

3 red peppers
olive oil
1 large red onion, peeled and cut into wedges
1 medium fennel bulb, trimmed and cut
into wedges
3 cloves of garlic, crushed, peeled and sliced
sea salt
freshly ground black pepper
200g goat's cheese

Heat the oven to 120°C/gas ¹/₂.
Cut the peppers in half and remove and discard
the entire core. Lightly oil a baking tray and place
the peppers on it.
　Put the onion, fennel and garlic in a bowl,
drizzle over some olive oil and add seasoning.
Mix to coat the vegetables in oil and seasoning,
and then divide them among the peppers,
stuffing them inside the pepper halves. Bake for
1 hour 20 minutes.
　Remove the stuffed peppers from the oven
and increase the heat to 190°C/gas 5. Slice the
goat's cheese and arrange it over the peppers.
Return the tray to the oven and roast for
5 minutes, until the cheese is bubbling.

Desserts

The names of French desserts are a translator's nightmare: *le gâteau* is a generic term for 'cake', although perplexingly, *le cake* refers to a kind of tea bread. The word *tarte* covers a wide variety of recipes, from the open fruit tarts to the upside-down Tarte Tatin, but there is no true word for 'pie' – unless we count *tourte*, which is most often used as a term of abuse. And as for translating some of the bizarre names of the confections to be found in French *pâtisseries* – it is almost impossible. Many of them are religious in origin – Saint-Honoré has a cake named after him, filled with whipped cream and sugar.

But the French have a long-standing tradition of irreverence towards the Catholic Church which extends even into the kitchen. How else can we explain the *religieuse* – that little cake made up of two choux buns one on top of the other, so that it looks like a fat little nun? Or even the deliciously named *pet de nonne*? These small, chocolate-coated pastries are now served under a respectable alias in some of our more elegant restaurants, but the original name – still gleefully used in many regions of France – translates as 'the nun's fart'. Remember that, next time you eat a profiterole.

It is a peculiar fact that the French, who make the most wonderful cakes, rarely eat dessert on a day-to-day basis. Fruit, yoghurt and cheese are the most usual endings to a meal, but on Sundays and during special celebrations, desserts really come into their own.

Blueberry Tart

Blueberries are plump, cultivated berries, which develop a great taste when cooked. Bilberries are tiny and grow wild in Europe, and have a sharp, tart flavour. The two are sometimes confused because of the similarity of the names. I like to make this tart with bilberries – *Tarte aux Myrtilles* – which are hard to find but worth it (this is the only thing that motivates me to brave the moors and pick a batch once in a while), but you can use any berry fruit in season; and besides blueberries, which the tart shown here is made from, blackberries, raspberries, blackcurrants and tayberries all work well. The *pâte brisée* is crumbly and light, like freshly baked biscuit, and although it is very easy to prepare, this is the kind of dessert that always gives me a sense of achievement.

Preparation: 40 minutes plus 1 hour's chilling
Cooking: 35 minutes

Serves 6

For the *pâte brisée*:
250g flour
175g butter, cut into small knobs, plus extra for greasing
20g unrefined caster sugar
1 egg
1/2 tbsp water

For the filling:
500g blueberries or other berries, stalks removed
2 eggs
125g unrefined caster sugar, plus extra for sprinkling
175ml double cream
25g flour
1 dessertspoonful *crème de cassis*

Rub the flour and butter together with your fingertips until the mixture looks like breadcrumbs. It really helps to work in a cool kitchen and have cool fingers. Mix in the sugar. Then add the egg and water, using a round-ended knife in a cutting motion to combine the ingredients until they form into a pastry ball. Put the pastry ball on to a cool, floured work surface and lightly knead with the palm of your hand for a minute, to ensure a smooth pastry. Wrap and place in the fridge to rest for 40 minutes.

Lightly butter a 25cm push-up-bottom flan tin. Dust a cool surface with flour and roll out the chilled pastry to more than fit the tin (because you do not want to have to stretch it). As this is a high-butter-content pastry, take care not to let the pastry stick to the surface – keep dusting lightly with flour. Line the tin with the rolled-out pastry with the excess lying over the edges, and to trim it, simply roll the pin over the flan tin. Return the pastry to the fridge for 20 minutes.

Heat the oven to 200°C/gas 6.

Place the berries in the chilled pastry case. Mix together the eggs, sugar, cream, flour and cassis until smooth and pour over the fruit. Lightly sprinkle with a little extra sugar and bake for 35 minutes. Serve cold, if you can wait.

You find fruit tarts like this one in all the most elegant *pâtisseries* in France; my mother used to buy them for birthdays and saint's days, but they are far too good to be kept for special occasions.

Strawberry Tart

This spectacular tart, *Tarte aux Fraises*, can also be made with any other fresh fruit – try raspberries, gages, peaches or apricots – and it looks terrific every time. These desserts were what I always had on festival days as a child, and their jewel colours and wonderful textures and scents will give an instant carnival atmosphere to any table. These tarts don't keep well, so eat on the same day: though who could not? Serve with thick cream.

Preparation: 40 minutes plus 1 hour's chilling
Cooking: 45 minutes

Serves 6

For the almond pastry:
225g flour
75g ground almonds
200g butter, cut into small knobs,
plus extra for greasing
150g unrefined light brown sugar
2–3 egg yolks

For the filling:
200g redcurrant jelly
1kg strawberries

Mix together the flour and ground almonds. Rub the butter into the flour with your fingertips until it resembles breadcrumbs. (Remember: cool kitchen and cool fingers, if you can.) Mix in the sugar. Then add the egg yolks and mix them in using a round-ended knife in a cutting motion until the ingredients come together into a pastry ball. Put the pastry ball on to a cool, floured work surface and lightly knead with the palm of your hand for a minute, to ensure a smooth pastry. Wrap and place in the fridge to rest for 40 minutes.

Lightly butter a 25cm push-up-bottom flan tin. Roll out the pastry on a lightly floured surface, then line the tin. Place in the fridge to chill again for 20 minutes.

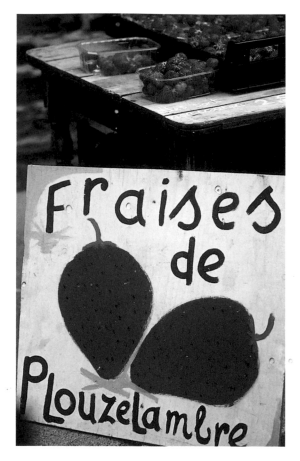

Heat the oven to 180°C/gas 4.

Line the pastry case with baking parchment and baking beans and bake for 20 minutes. Then remove the lining paper and beans, reduce the heat to 150°C/gas 2, and bake for a further 25 minutes until the pastry is golden and set. Remove from the oven and allow to cool.

Gently heat the redcurrant jelly in a small saucepan over a low heat until thin and smooth. Allow the jelly to cool a little.

Carefully release the cooled pastry case and transfer it to a large flat plate. Do take care, as this pastry is fragile. Cut any large strawberries into smaller pieces, then pile the fruit into the case. Spoon the redcurrant jelly over the strawberries to give an even coating, leave to set for 1 hour, then serve.

Lemon Tart

This is my great-aunt Simone's version of an old and well-loved dish, *Tarte au Citron*. I love it: the creamy filling has an intense, sunny flavour, and I like it best in winter, when I eat it to counteract seasonal blues. It's one of Anouchka's favourite desserts, too, and it's easy enough to make that she can help me. I have to watch her carefully, though – she eats the lemons when I'm not looking!

Preparation: 40 minutes plus 1 hour's chilling
Cooking: 35 minutes

Serves 6

For the *pâte brisée*:
250g flour
175g butter, cut into small knobs
20g unrefined caster sugar
1 egg
2 tsp water

For the filling:
2 eggs
100g unrefined sugar
150ml double cream
zest and juice of 2 lemons
50g butter

Rub the flour and butter together with your fingertips until the mixture looks like breadcrumbs. (A cool kitchen and cool fingers help.) Mix in the sugar. Add the egg and water and mix it in using a round-ended knife in a cutting motion until the ingredients come together into a dough ball.

Put the pastry ball on to a cool, floured work surface and lightly knead with the palm of your hand for a minute, to ensure a smooth pastry. Wrap and place in the fridge to rest for 40 minutes.

Lightly butter a 25cm push-up-bottom flan tin. Roll out the pastry on a lightly floured surface, then line the tin. Trim the edges with a knife and return to the fridge for 20 minutes to chill and relax.

Heat the oven to 180°C/gas 4.

Put the eggs, sugar, double cream and lemon zest and juice into a bowl and whisk well until creamy. Melt the butter and whisk it into the lemon mixture, then pour it into the chilled pastry case.

Carefully place the tart in the oven and bake for 15 minutes, then reduce the heat to 160°C/gas 3 and bake for a further 20 minutes or until the filling has set. Leave to cool for 1 hour before serving.

Grandmother's Festival Loaf

This is a lovely loaf, half bread, half cake, traditionally from the Auvergne region, hence its name: *Fouace Aveyronnaise.*

Preparation: 30 minutes, plus 2 hours' proving
Cooking: 30 minutes

Serves 6

120ml milk
7g yeast and a pinch of sugar
375g flour
50g butter, softened
1 tbsp orange flower water or rum
40g unrefined sugar
2 eggs, plus 1 egg, beaten, for glazing
100g crystallized fruits, chopped

Barely warm the milk, just to remove the chill, then sprinkle in the yeast and sugar and leave to sit for a few minutes.

Place the flour, butter, orange flower water or rum, sugar, eggs and yeast-and-milk mixture in a large bowl and mix well. Add the crystallized fruit and then turn the dough out on to a lightly floured surface. Knead for 8 minutes.

Return the dough to the bowl, cover, and keep in a warm place for 1 hour. The mixture should double in size.

Turn out the dough on to a floured surface again and knead until the dough is soft and elastic. Lightly butter a baking sheet and dust it with flour. Shape the dough into a long sausage, join the two ends together into a circle, place it on the baking tray, glaze with egg and leave it to rest for 1 hour.

Heat the oven to 200°C/gas 6. Just before placing the loaf in the oven glaze it with egg again. Cook for 30 minutes until golden brown.

I find bread-making extremely therapeutic, and this
finished loaf looks beautiful, like a summer garland
studded with colourful pieces of crystallized fruit.
I like to make it on Midsummer's Eve, and eat it out
in the garden with cheese, fruit and honey.

Breton Flan

This typical Breton flan, *Far Breton*, is a favourite emergency dessert, and all the members of my family have a different version of it. This one belongs to Juliette Jeuland of Châteaubourg, and uses the traditional prunes, but you can also use dried apricots, cherries, berries or raisins soaked in Armagnac.

Preparation: 10 minutes
Cooking: 30 minutes

Serves 6

3 eggs
100g unrefined light brown sugar,
plus extra for dusting
125g flour
500ml milk
80g butter, plus extra for greasing
150g pitted prunes

Heat the oven to 180°C/gas 4.
Mix together the eggs, sugar and flour in a bowl until smooth and blended.
Warm the milk and butter until the butter has melted, then add to the flour mixture and blend together well. Finally, stir in the prunes.
Butter a low-sided earthenware dish and pour the prune mixture into it. Cook for 30 minutes, until risen and browned on top. Dust with sugar, and serve warm or cold.

Gâteau Breton

This is a traditional Breton cake with a rich, buttery taste and a slightly 'sandy' texture, like that of the *sablé* biscuits of the region. Everyone has their own private way of doing it. This is the plain recipe, from Danielle Stéphan of Trégastel, but you can fill your gâteau with raspberry jam, prunes or liqueur-soaked fruit for a moist, luxurious version.

Preparation: 30 minutes
Cooking: 35 minutes

Serves 6

200g flour
50g soft butter, cut into small knobs,
plus extra for greasing
200g unrefined caster sugar
zest of 1 orange
5 egg yolks
milk for glazing

Heat the oven to 160°C/gas 3. Generously butter a 24cm push-up-bottom cake tin.
Place the flour in a bowl, add the butter, sugar, orange zest and egg yolks, and work together with your fingers until all the ingredients are evenly blended – the mixture will be quite sticky. Put the mixture into the prepared cake tin and spread it out with your hands.
Make a pattern in the top of the cake mixture with a knife or pastry cutter, and brush the surface with a little milk. Bake for 35 minutes, until the cake is golden brown and has come away from the sides of the tin.
Leave to cool in the tin for 5 minutes before turning out.

Tarte Tatin

This beautifully golden, caramelized tart is best served warm, but not too hot, so that the flavours really get the chance to develop. It is a wonderful autumn recipe for home-grown apples, such as Cox's Orange Pippins – or Bramley's, if you prefer something with a little more bite.

Preparation: 35 minutes plus 30 minutes' chilling
Cooking: 55 minutes

Serves 6

For the pastry:
150g flour, plus extra for dusting
100g butter, cut into small knobs
25g unrefined caster sugar
2 egg yolks

For the apples:
100g unrefined caster sugar
40g butter
5 eating apples, peeled, cored and quartered

To make the pastry, rub together the flour and butter with your fingertips until it resembles breadcrumbs. Mix in the sugar.

Add the egg yolks and, with a round-bladed knife, use a cutting motion to mix until the breadcrumbs gather together to form a ball. Turn the pastry ball out on to a floured surface, dust your hands with a little flour and knead the pastry together until smooth.

Wrap and chill in the fridge for 30 minutes. Place a 20–25cm ovenproof frying pan over a medium heat, and melt the butter and sugar until syrupy.

Heat the oven to 200°C/gas 6.

Arrange the apple quarters in the frying pan and cook for 15 minutes: this gives the golden colour to the apples and allows the sugar to turn to caramel.

Roll out the pastry on a lightly floured surface to a size slightly greater than the frying pan. Remove the frying pan from the heat and quickly lay the pastry over the apples, tucking in any excess around the edges. Place in the oven and cook for 20 minutes, then reduce the heat to 160°C/gas 3 and cook for a further 20 minutes.

Remove from the oven and gently ease a knife all the way around the edge of the tart. Place a large heatproof plate upside down on top of the frying pan and quickly turn over the pan and plate, releasing the tart on to the plate. Lift off the frying pan to reveal golden brown apples and a syrupy sauce.

Hot puddings are a rarity in France, but this famous tart is one of the best. I particularly like it when it is very slightly burnt, so that the caramel develops a smoky flavour and the pastry a sticky, crispy texture. Perfect with good vanilla ice-cream.

Apple Slipper

This little flaky butter pastry, *Chausson aux Pommes*, is named for its shape. It is a favourite with children at *goûter*, the four o'clock snack that is traditional in France. Serve it warm.

Preparation: 2 hours plus 1 hour's chilling
Cooking: 1 hour

Serves 6

250g cold butter
250g flour, plus extra for dusting
75ml cold water
500g apples, peeled, cored and diced
25g unrefined caster sugar, plus extra for dusting
1/2 tsp cinnamon
1 beaten egg for sealing

Take 200g of the butter, hard from the fridge, and cut it into very small pieces. Place the pieces on a tray and leave to soften for 20 minutes.

Put the flour in a bowl, add a few pieces of butter and toss them in the flour using a round-bladed knife. Continue adding butter until all of it is well coated in flour, so that no pieces get the chance to clump together. Add the cold water and with a cutting motion quickly mix until the pastry comes together into a ball.

Transfer to a lightly dusted, cool surface and gently shape with your hands into a brick. Roll out to an oblong about 18 x 10cm. Fold one third over to the centre, the other third over that, then use the rolling pin to press the edges together, trapping pockets of air. Let it rest for 5 minutes.

Lightly flour the surface again, give the pastry a quarter turn, and repeat as above. Do this three more times. Wrap and chill for 1 hour.

Melt the remaining 50g butter in a large frying pan over a moderate heat, add the apples and cook gently for 5 minutes. Stir in the sugar and cinnamon, remove from the heat and allow to cool completely.

Heat the oven to 190°C/gas 5.

Dust a baking sheet with flour and roll out the pastry to a circle about 1cm thick. Spoon the apples into one half, brush the edges with egg and fold the pastry over into a half-moon shape. Crimp the edges with your fingers to seal them. Brush with egg , pierce with a fork and dust with sugar. Bake for 20 minutes. Reduce the heat to 160°F/gas 3 and bake for 20 minutes more.

Cherry Clafoutis

This simple pudding can also be made with other soft fruits, such as apricots, plums, peaches, blackberries and blackcurrants.

Preparation: 45 minutes
(due to pitting of fresh cherries)
Cooking: 40 minutes

Serves 6

15g butter for greasing
750g cherries, pitted
125g flour
50g unrefined caster sugar
3 eggs
1 tsp vanilla extract
300ml milk
unrefined icing sugar for dusting

Heat the oven to 180°C/gas 4. Butter a shallow ovenproof dish. Place the cherries in the dish.

Put the flour and sugar in a large bowl and make a well in the middle. Whisk the eggs; add the vanilla and milk to the eggs and whisk. Slowly pour the milk mix into the flour, beating constantly until all the liquid has been added and you have a smooth batter. Pour over the cherries.

Bake for 40 minutes until the batter is firm to the touch and golden on top. Sprinkle with icing sugar and serve just warm.

This is a summer favourite with children – although the grown-up version, with the addition of kirsch, also goes down rather well. I got this recipe from my aunt Claudine, whose cherry trees I remember with great affection.

Braised Cherries with Spiced Toasts

The French name is *Soupe aux Cerises*, though this is not quite what we expect from a soup.

Preparation: 40 minutes
Cooking: 20 minutes

Serves 6

500g black cherries, pitted
2 tbsp unrefined sugar
1 tbsp kirsch (for adults)
75g butter
10 slices of baguette
50g unrefined sugar
1 tsp cinnamon
$^1/_2$ tbsp flour

Place the cherries, sugar and kirsch in a saucepan over a medium heat. Bring to the boil, then reduce the heat and simmer for 15 minutes.

Heat the butter in a frying pan and fry the slices of baguette on each side until golden.

Remove the bread, dust with sugar and cinnamon, and place at the bottom of a serving dish. When the cherries are soft and cooked, remove them from the juice and pile on to the bread.

Blend the flour with a little water and, using a balloon whisk, quickly mix this into the warm cherry juice. Gently bring to the boil. The mixture will thicken slightly, becoming velvety. Pour over the bread and cherries, and serve.

Chantilly Meringues

These light and fluffy meringues are perfect with fruit, such as a bowl of fresh summer berries, or the Slow Fudge Sauce on this page, or a drizzle of chocolate fondue (page 233): or perhaps more than one of these …

Preparation: 15 minutes
Cooking: 2 hours (or more)

Serves 6

For the meringues:
3 egg whites
180g unrefined caster sugar

For the crème Chantilly:
300ml double cream
25g unrefined caster sugar
few drops vanilla extract

Heat the oven to 140°C/gas 1.
Place the egg whites in a mixing bowl and beat with an electric whisk until stiff. (Or whisk by hand … until stiff.) Beat in half the sugar, then add the remaining sugar and beat.

Line a baking tray with baking parchment and scoop the meringue mixture on to the paper in 12 spoonfuls. Bake for 2 hours. For perfect crisp and dry meringues, turn the oven off but leave the meringues to cool in there for a further 12 hours.

Whisk the cream with the sugar and vanilla extract until it stands in soft peaks. Scoop cream on to 6 of the meringues, then sandwich the other 6 meringues on top of these. Chill before serving.

Slow Fudge Sauce

This tantalizingly slow fudge sauce – Caramel Marie Sorin, from my great-aunt Marinette – is a luxury for those days when ice cream alone just isn't enough. Part of the pleasure of this recipe is the time it takes to prepare it and the anticipation that goes with it. By the time it is ready, the entire house smells like a sweet shop, spirits have magically lifted and even the rain has stopped. If you have some left (this has never happened to me yet), then line a tin with baking paper, pour in the sauce and leave it to set in the fridge for a couple of hours. Then cut into squares for a smooth and creamy fudge.

Preparation: 5 minutes
Cooking: 30 minutes

Serves 6

500g unrefined sugar
10g butter
400g tin condensed milk
75ml milk

Put all the ingredients in a heavy-based pan and cook over a very low heat, stirring constantly until all the sugar has melted. You must stir constantly, otherwise the sugar will burn and the sauce becomes inedible. Slowly bring to the boil, and simmer very gently for 20 minutes, continuing to stir all the while.

Remove from the heat and beat well with a wooden spoon. Serve warm with a really good vanilla ice cream.

Crème Brûlée

This is a quick and easy version of a perennial favourite – try adding a handful of redcurrants or raspberries to the mixture for a fresh, summery variation. Make this a day before serving it to get a really firm set.

Preparation: 15 minutes, plus overnight chilling
Cooking: 20 minutes

Serves 6

1 vanilla pod
375ml double cream
5 egg yolks
25g unrefined caster sugar
unrefined icing sugar, to serve

Cut the vanilla pod in half lengthways, scrape out the seeds and put them in a small saucepan with the cream. Discard the pod. Gently bring the cream to a simmer – do not boil – then remove from the heat.

Heat the oven to 160°C/gas 3.

In a bowl, beat together the egg yolks and caster sugar until light and fluffy. Stir in the warmed cream and mix well.

Make a bain-marie. Place the mixing bowl over a saucepan of simmering water on a gentle heat, stirring constantly until the mixture coats the back of the spoon: about 8 minutes.

Pour the custard into individual ramekins (or you could use one large ovenproof serving dish).

Make a bain-marie with a deep roasting tin: place the dishes in the tin and half-fill the tin with hot water. Place it in the oven and cook the custards for 20 minutes. Remove and allow to cool, then place in the fridge overnight.

The next day, heat the grill to high. Sieve the icing sugar over the custards and place under the grill. The sugar will melt and caramelize. Move the dishes around so that they brown evenly. Leave to cool completely before serving.

Crème Caramel

This is one of my favourite desserts. No two people make it in exactly the same way, but this is my grandmother's recipe, and ideally it should be made 24 hours in advance to give the rich caramel colour at the bottom of the dish time to develop.

Preparation: 20 minutes, plus 1 hour or overnight chilling
Cooking: 1 hour

Serves 6

For the caramel:
200g unrefined caster sugar
50ml water

For the cream:
500ml milk
3 eggs
2 egg yolks
60g unrefined sugar
a few drops of vanilla extract

Heat the oven to 160°C/gas 3. Place an ovenproof soufflé dish in the oven to warm.

Make the caramel. Place the sugar and water in a small pan. Bring to the boil, then simmer until golden brown. Pour into the warm soufflé dish.

Place the milk in a pan and bring gently to the boil. Take off the heat.

Mix together the eggs, egg yolks, sugar and vanilla extract in a bowl. Pour this into the hot milk and stir well. Strain the mixture through a fine sieve into the caramel-lined soufflé dish.

Make a bain-marie: place the dish in a deep roasting tin and half-fill the tin with hot water. Carefully place in the oven and cook for 1 hour. Remove and allow to cool, then place in the fridge for an hour before serving (or overnight).

To turn out the caramel, run a knife around the custard. Place a deep-sided serving plate over the top and invert the dish into the plate. Carefully remove the soufflé dish, and serve.

Kirsch Soufflé

Soufflé means 'blown', like glass, and people tend to think that soufflés are delicate and tricky to make. This isn't true; it's a quick, light, versatile dish – just avoid opening the oven door while your soufflé is cooking, and eat it straight away once cooked. This shouldn't be a problem – it's irresistible!

Preparation: 20 minutes
Cooking: 15 minutes

Serves 6

butter for greasing
2 tbsp unrefined caster sugar
50g flour
200ml milk
75g unrefined sugar
20g butter
4 egg yolks
125ml kirsch
7 egg whites

Heat the oven to 190°C/gas 5.

Take a 20cm soufflé dish – or 6 individual ramekins – and lightly rub with a little butter, then coat with a layer of sugar. Roll the dish(es) around until evenly coated with the sugar.

Place the flour in a bowl, add a little milk and work to form a smooth paste.

Heat the remaining milk, sugar and butter in a saucepan. When this reaches the boil, slowly pour it into the flour paste, whisking with a balloon whisk until the mixture is smooth. Return the mixture to the pan and bring to the boil, stirring constantly. Remove from the heat and add the egg yolks and kirsch, mixing well until smooth.

Beat the egg whites in a large bowl with an electric whisk until stiff. Add the kirsch mixture to the whites and fold in quickly until evenly blended. Carefully pour into the prepared soufflé dish or dishes, put immediately into the oven and cook for 10 minutes.

Without removing the soufflé from the oven, dust with icing sugar and cook for a further 5 minutes. Serve immediately on warmed plates.

There are plenty of variations for this easy dish – try using Grand Marnier, chartreuse or rum for a change, and serve with a sweet, fruity wine such as Sauternes or Monbazillac.

Ripe pears just off the tree have almost nothing in common with the hard, green ones you find in some supermarkets. Choose a firm, slightly floury species (such as Williams), which will really absorb the flavours of the wine and spices.

Pears Poached in Red Wine

Poires au Vin Rouge is a terrific way of preparing autumn pears, and fills the house with a marvellous scent of wine and spices. The juice makes a wonderful spicy punch – just add a little cognac!

Preparation: 25 minutes
Cooking: 30 minutes

Serves 6

1 bottle red Burgundy
4 cloves
2 blades of mace
100g unrefined caster sugar
6 pears

Place the red wine, cloves, mace and caster sugar in a saucepan (large enough also to accommodate the pears) and gently bring to a simmer.

Peel the pears, carefully keeping their beautiful shape and the stem on. Add the pears to the wine and simmer for 30 minutes, turning the pears to ensure even cooking and staining from the red wine.

Leave the pears to cool in the wine and then serve at room temperature. The pears can be served on their own or in a soup bowl with a ladleful of the red wine.

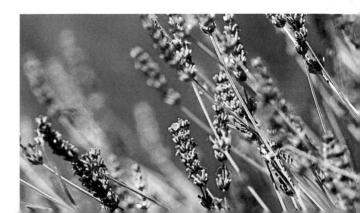

Pear and Chocolate Brioche Pudding

Brioche is a lovely soft roll or loaf made from a yeast dough enriched with eggs and butter, which give it its distinctive colour and flavour. Brioche varies in shape from region to region, with the Parisian variety – a small ball of brioche on top of a larger base, or *brioche à tête* – perhaps most familiar to us. The most highly regarded brioches come from Gournay and Gisors in Normandy. Serve with scoops of real vanilla ice cream for a melt-in-your-mouth pudding.

Preparation: 25 minutes plus 40 minutes' resting
Cooking: 45 minutes

Serves 6

butter for greasing
300g brioche, sliced
5 ripe pears, peeled and sliced
450ml cream
450ml milk
100g chocolate (70 per cent cocoa)
50g unrefined caster sugar, plus extra for sprinkling
3 eggs

Butter a low-sided ovenproof dish. Arrange the slices of brioche and pear alternately in the dish. Warm the cream and milk in a saucepan over a low heat. Break the chocolate into small pieces, add it to the warm milk and cream along with the sugar, and stir until melted. Do not boil. Whisk the eggs and mix them into the warm chocolatey milk, then pour the liquid over the brioche and pear slices, wetting the entire brioche. Press down with a spatula, and leave to stand for 40 minutes.

Heat the oven to 160°C/gas 3.
Sprinkle the pudding with a little extra sugar, and place it in a bain-marie (that is, place the baking dish in a large roasting tin and fill the tin with hot water to come halfway up the pudding dish).

Place in the oven and cook for 45 minutes until soft and golden.

Polenta Pudding Cake

This warm polenta-based pudding cake, *Gâteau Francesca*, is lovely cold-weather comfort food.

Preparation: 20 minutes
Cooking: 30 minutes

Serves 6

250g butter, plus extra for greasing
250g unrefined caster sugar
3 unwaxed lemons
4 eggs
125g polenta
25g ground almonds
100g flour
cream, to serve

Heat the oven to 160°C/gas 3. Lightly butter a 20cm pie dish.

Cream together the butter and caster sugar with an electric whisk until soft and smooth. Finely grate the lemon zest from two and a half of the lemons and then juice them. Add the zest and juice to the cake mix and blend. Thinly slice the remaining half a lemon and keep on one side.

Beat the eggs into the cake mix –it will split, but do not worry, this is normal. Then beat in the polenta and ground almonds. Finally, fold in the flour with a large spoon.

Transfer the cake mix to the buttered dish, arrange the lemon slices on top and bake for 25–30 minutes. Serve warm, with cream.

Mémée's Cherries

Of all my great-grandmother's recipes, this is the one I remember best. She gave my mother several jars of these preserved cherries when my mother came to England, and there are still some left, a precious few, in a big jar at the bottom of the liqueur cabinet. On special occasions, we drink a little of the liqueur, with a single cherry at the bottom of the glass. The cherries are forty years old now, and they have macerated for so long that even the stones – and the little nut inside – are infused with the flavour of the Armagnac. You can use the same basic recipe for almost any fruit: raspberries, small plums, blackberries, redcurrants. You can vary the alcohol, too; any kind of clear spirit works well, including vodka or white rum. I make my own now, although I still like Mémée's best. Perhaps in another forty years …

Preparation: 30 minutes
Steeping: up to forty years!

Serves 6

sour cherries
Armagnac
unrefined caster sugar
a pinch of cinnamon
you also need a Mason sealable jar

Choose undamaged sour cherries of very good quality. Wash the cherries and leave the stones in. Cut off part of the stem only with scissors.

Put 3 layers of cherries at the bottom of the jar. Top with 2 to 3 tablespoons of caster sugar. Add a pinch of cinnamon. Repeat this process till you are close to the top of the jar, then cover with about 2cm of sugar. Top with spirit so that the fruit is covered. Seal the jar.

Turn the jar a few times to dissolve the sugar. Turn again in a few days' time.

Consume after a few months (the longer you wait, the better the result).

Sloe Gin and Mango Crush

This makes a delicious and wickedly refreshing end to a rich meal.

Preparation: 25 minutes
Freezing: 70 minutes

Serves 6

3 large ripe mangoes
50ml gin
50ml sloe gin
50g dark chocolate (70 per cent cocoa),
cut into small pieces

Place 6 glasses in the freezer.

Peel the skin away from the mango with a sharp knife, then cut all the flesh away from the stone and roughly chop it. Place it in a bowl and blend with a hand-held blender until the mixture is a purée. Add the gin and sloe gin and mix well.

Place in the freezer for 1 hour and then remove and break up the crystals with a fork. Return to the freezer and chill for 10 minutes before again breaking up the crystals with a fork.

Repeat this process at least 5 or 6 times, or until the crystals are firm enough to hold their shape. Fill the chilled glasses with the crush and return it to the fridge for 10 minutes. Serve at once with a small nib of dark chocolate.

My brother came up with this delicious and unusual dessert – so simple, and yet so good! My daughter prefers the alcohol-free version, topped with a cherry and curls of milk chocolate.

Chocolate

I have to admit that for a while after writing *Chocolat* I felt that I would never be able to eat chocolate again. After months of chocolate festivals, chocolate premières, chocolate factories, chocolate-themed parties and openings and dinners, after being on the set of the film, where even the wood shavings smelt of chocolate, I think even the most devoted chocolate addict might have begun to feel rather sated. I was disgusted, chocced-out, finished.

The Italians saved me; as I arrived at yet another chocolate event, this time in the exquisite coffee-shop and *chocolaterie* of Cova, in Milan, I was greeted by the owner, who, taking one look at my pale, exhausted face, smiled and said: 'Wait here. I have something special for you to try.' As he vanished into a back room, I tried to school my features (for the thousandth time) into an expression of blissful surprise: *Chocolate! My favourite!*

I felt my worst suspicions about to be confirmed when the gentleman returned carrying a silver tray – which on closer examination revealed a generous pile of the most incredible, delicious, vocabulary-challengingly excellent anchovy toasts I have ever eaten. I spent that blissful afternoon gorging on anchovy toasts and plump black olives, and when I got home again I found that my chocolate aversion had magically disappeared. I was cured.

As a result, when we were compiling this book we found that the chocolate recipes outnumbered the rest to such an extent that we decided to create an entirely separate section devoted to this uniquely versatile and enchanting substance. Some of the recipes are from *Chocolat* – the ones you keep asking me for – and some are old (or new) favourites gathered along the way.

To my great disappointment, the gentleman from Cova refused to give me the exact recipe for the life-saving anchovy toasts, but you can make a good approximation of it using the tapenade recipe on page 59.

Chocolate: a unique substance. It can be melted, grated, sculpted and spun. It can be eaten in savouries as well as sweets with equal pleasure, or just devoured on its own. Bliss.

Tempering Chocolate

Note for all chocolates-lovers: never store chocolate in the fridge or cool it in the fridge.

Couverture is also called dipping or coating chocolate, and professional chocolate makers always use it. It comes in all varieties, but has a high cocoa butter content, thus making it ideal for hand-made chocolates. The best couverture comes from France, Belgium and Switzerland. Couverture needs to be tempered in order to give it a perfectly smooth and glossy finish.

Tempering is really very simple, and although it takes a little time, it is worth the effort to achieve a really professional gloss. You will need a sugar thermometer, and then all the process requires is to take the couverture to a certain temperature and then to cool it. This changes the crystalline structure of the chocolate and makes it shiny and manageable.

If the idea of tempering chocolate really doesn't appeal, you can simply melt good quality eating chocolate using the bain-marie method. It tastes fine, although your chocolate will not have the shiny, professional texture or the 'snap' of tempered couverture.

To temper chocolate:
First break the chocolate into small pieces. If it comes from a professional supplier it may already come as buttons.

Place the chocolate in a heatproof dish. Make a bain-marie by standing the dish in a pan of simmering water over a low heat, and warm through, stirring occasionally.

Then, when the chocolate reaches 45°C, remove the dish from the bain-marie and stand it in a pan of cold water. Mix well and allow the temperature to drop back to 25°C.

Finally, return the dish to the hot bain-marie, mix well and heat the chocolate to 30°C.

The chocolate has now been tempered and is ready for use.

Mendiants

These are my own favourites – little discs of chocolate sprinkled with whatever you like best: almonds, candied lemon peel, glacé cherries, walnuts or fat Malaga raisins. Anouchka likes to do the artistic part (while I do most of the eating). The name means 'beggars'. Traditionally served at Christmas with toppings of dried fruit and nuts in four colours, they were meant to represent the four Roman Catholic mendicant orders (white for the Dominicans, grey for the Franciscans, brown for the Carmelites and deep purple for the Augustines).

Preparation: 1 hour
Setting: 1 hour

Makes about 65

500g milk or dark couverture, tempered as on page 216
150g of your combined choice of almonds, walnuts, raisins, sultanas, candied fruits

Place teaspoonfuls of the couverture on a large sheet of baking parchment. Gently spread each one with the back of the spoon to make a 2.5cm-diameter circle. Scatter the fruits and nuts on top of the discs and allow to cool.

Apricot Truffles

The slight sharpness of the apricot provides a delicious contrast to the dark chocolate in these luscious truffles.

Preparation: 2 hours
Setting: 1 hour

Makes about 36

450g milk chocolate (70 per cent cocoa)
170ml milk
1 tbsp apricot liqueur
12 soft dried apricots, finely diced
100g milk couverture
200g cocoa powder

Put the chocolate in a heatproof bowl. Place in a bain-marie (over a saucepan of simmering water), and mix until melted. Heat the milk in a small saucepan until boiling. Pour into the melted chocolate and stir well. Add the liqueur and blend until smooth.

Remove from the heat. Gradually add the apricot pieces, stirring constantly. As the mixture cools it will thicken and form a workable paste. Allow to cool so that you can roll the mixture into balls between your fingers. Leave to cool completely, while you temper the couverture for dipping (see page 216).

Sift the cocoa powder on to a plate. Using a thin fork, stab the truffles one at a time, dip in the tempered chocolate, then roll in the cocoa powder and leave to cool.

Left to right are untipped Nipples of Venus,
Mendiants, finished Nipples of Venus (see page
220) and Apricot Truffles. For a shortcut version of
the truffles, don't bother with the couverture and
simply roll the truffles in cocoa powder.

Nipples of Venus

This was originally an Italian confection, but I put it in because I couldn't resist the name …

Preparation: 2 hours
Setting: 1 hour

Makes about 70

For the filling:
225g dark chocolate (70 per cent cocoa)
300ml double cream

For dipping:
100g dark chocolate (70 per cent cocoa)
50g white chocolate

For the filling, break the chocolate into small pieces and place in a heatproof bowl. Make a bain-marie (put the bowl over a saucepan of simmering water) and allow the chocolate to melt. Heat the cream in a small saucepan and add it to the melted chocolate, mixing until evenly blended. Leave to cool for 2 hours. Then, using an electric whisk, beat until the mixture becomes stiff and holds its shape.

Line 3 baking trays with baking parchment. Put the filling mixture into a piping bag with a 1cm plain nozzle and pipe little mounds – or nipples – on to the baking parchment. Put in the fridge to chill and set.

Melt the dark chocolate in a bain-marie. Take each chilled nipple and dip in the melted dark chocolate. Return to the parchment paper and leave to set for an hour.

Melt the white chocolate in a bain-marie. Take each dark-chocolate-covered nipple and dip the tip into the white chocolate. Leave to set. Enjoy!

Chocolate Pot

This is pure indulgence of the highest order. Try adding finely grated orange zest, or a dash of brandy, whisky or Kahlua, to make your own personal pot.

Preparation: 25 minutes
Chilling: overnight

Serves 6

250g dark chocolate (70 per cent cocoa)
750ml double cream
6 chocolate scrolls or 6 teaspoons crème fraiche, to serve

Break the chocolate into small pieces and put in a heatproof bowl. Place in a bain-marie (over a saucepan of simmering water) until almost melted. Heat the cream in a saucepan until just simmering, then add to the melted chocolate and blend until a smooth thick sauce has formed.

Pour into small ramekins or glasses, and leave to chill in the fridge overnight. Garnish with a chocolate scroll or a teaspoon of crème fraiche.

This is Lawrence's chocolate cake (see over): a cake so rich you can only serve it in slivers! Always line the tin with baking parchment (not greaseproof paper) to ensure you can easily release this rich, moist cake.

Gâteau Lawrence

This is a rich cake. If you find, as I do, that the chocolate icing seems a little too much of a good thing, try drizzling about 6 tablespoons of warmed apricot jam over the cake just before serving – the sharp tang of the fruit makes a wonderful contrast to the dark chocolate. Bliss!

Preparation: 30 minutes
Cooking: 50 minutes

Serves 6

For the cake:
180g dark chocolate (70 per cent cocoa)
175g butter, softened
125g unrefined sugar
200g ground almonds
4 eggs, separated

For the icing:
100g dark chocolate (70 per cent cocoa)
50g butter

Heat the oven to 150°C/gas 2.

Line a 25cm push-up-bottom or springform cake tin with baking parchment.

Break the chocolate into pieces and melt it in a bain-marie (that is, in a heatproof bowl over a pan of simmering water).

Cream together the butter and sugar until soft and creamy, using an electric whisk if you have one. Add the ground almonds, egg yolks and melted chocolate, and beat until evenly blended.

Whisk the egg whites until stiff, add to the cake mixture and quickly fold in until evenly mixed using a large metal spoon. Pour into the prepared cake tin and bake for 35 minutes. A light crust will form on the top and the middle should still be a little squishy. Leave to cool a little before carefully removing from the tin.

For the icing, melt the chocolate and butter in a bain-marie, drizzle over the cake and leave to set.

My brother Lawrence discovered this luscious chocolate cake, which uses ground almonds instead of flour for an incredibly moist and gooey consistency.

Anouchka's Chocolate Cake

My daughter usually prefers fresh mangoes to chocolate, but sometimes makes an exception in the case of this very special two-chocolate cake.

Preparation: 40 minutes
Cooking: 35 minutes

Serves 6

For the cake:
180g butter, softened
180g unrefined brown sugar
40g dark chocolate (70 per cent cocoa)
3 eggs
50g ground almonds
130g self-raising flour

For the icing:
190g unrefined icing sugar
25g butter, softened, cut into pieces
70ml hot milk
30g cocoa powder
20g white chocolate, grated
20g dark chocolate, grated

Heat the oven to 180°C/gas 4. Butter a 20cm push-up-bottom or springform cake tin.

Cream together the butter and sugar with an electric whisk until creamy and fluffy. Melt the chocolate in a bain-marie (that is, in a heatproof bowl over a pan of simmering water). Break the eggs into the butter and sugar one at a time and whisk. The mixture will split, but don't worry – it will come back once you add the flour. Add the melted chocolate and ground almonds and blend well. Fold in the flour with a large metal spoon, then transfer the mixture to the cake tin.

Bake for 35 minutes, or until the cake has come away from the sides of the tin, or a knife inserted into it comes out clean. Allow the cake to cool in the tin for 5 minutes before turning out. Then cool completely before icing it.

To make the icing, sift the icing sugar into a bowl, add the butter pieces and mix with a fork. In a separate small bowl, pour the milk over the cocoa powder and mix until dissolved, then add this to the icing sugar and blend. Spread over the cake and then decorate with grated chocolate.

No Bake Crunch Cake

I used to make this absurdly simple cake over my single gas-ring when I was at university, and leave it to chill on my window-ledge overnight. It got me through a lot of late-night revision crises, and it's a great way to use up broken biscuits.

Preparation: 25 minutes
Chilling: 2 hours

Serves 6

150g butter
3 tbsp golden syrup
1 tbsp black treacle
200g dark chocolate (70 per cent cocoa)
150g mixed dried sultanas or raisins
75g glacé cherries
75g dried apricots
150g mixed nuts and seeds, chopped
1 x 250g packet digestive biscuits
unrefined icing sugar for dusting

Line a square 23cm low-sided baking tin with baking parchment.

Carefully melt the butter, golden syrup, black treacle and chocolate in a saucepan over a low heat.

Place the sultanas or raisins, glacé cherries, apricots, nuts and seeds in a bowl.

Roughly crush the digestive biscuits (the best way is to place them in a strong plastic bag and break them up with a rolling pin) and add to the fruits in the bowl. Pour in the melted butter mix, stir, and transfer to the prepared tin. Smooth out and leave to set in the fridge for 2 hours.

Dust with icing sugar and then cut into fingers with a sharp knife.

Roulade Bicolore

This two-tone cake combines two kinds of chocolate for a melting contrast of flavours. Topped with chocolate curls, it makes a spectacular Yule log or celebration cake.

Preparation: 30 minutes
Cooking: 15 minutes

Serves 6

For the roulade:
60g dark chocolate (70 per cent cocoa)
50g butter
150g unrefined light muscovado sugar
2 eggs
1 tbsp Kahlua liqueur
2 tbsp milk
150g self-raising flour

For the filling:
250ml double cream
125g white chocolate, grated
1/2 tsp vanilla extract

For the decoration:
30g white chocolate, grated
30g dark chocolate (70 per cent cocoa), grated

Heat the oven to 180°C/gas 4.

Line a 36cm x 25cm tin with baking parchment. First make the roulade. Break the chocolate into pieces and melt in a bain-marie (that is, in a heatproof bowl over a pan of simmering water).

Place the butter and sugar in a bowl and whisk until creamy and fluffy using an electric whisk. Add the eggs and continue to beat – the mixture will split but this is normal. Pour in the melted chocolate and mix well. Add the Kahlua and milk, and mix until smooth. Fold in the flour, then place the mixture in the prepared tin and spread it out evenly. Bake for 10 minutes. Remove from the oven, take the cake out of the tin and leave to cool on a wire rack until cold.

To make the filling, whisk the cream until it stands in very soft peaks using an electric whisk. Lightly mix in the grated chocolate and vanilla. Take care not to overwhip the cream or it will lose its light, soft texture. Place the cooled roulade on the work surface, baking-parchment side down, and spread the filling on top, keeping a space clear all around the edge.

Use the parchment paper to help you roll up the roulade into a log. Wrap the paper around the roulade and shape it with your hands into a smooth log, allow to sit for 5 minutes, then transfer on to a serving plate, removing the paper. Top with dark and white chocolate shavings.

A roulade is a marvellous thing, but difficult to serve. A serrated knife is likely to break it up, so use a sharp fine knife to cut it, and a palette knife to help to hold it together.

Chocolate Cheesecake

It takes willpower to wait out the three-hour chilling time for this exceptional cheesecake – I find that I need an extra 200g of those chocolate-chip cookies to help me through it.

Preparation: 45minutes
Chilling: 3 hours

Serves 6

200g chocolate chip cookies, crushed
1/2 tsp cinnamon
100g butter, melted
100g dark chocolate (70 per cent cocoa)
1 tbsp Kahlua or Tia Maria liqueur
100g white chocolate
1 vanilla pod
225ml crème fraiche
75g unrefined demerara sugar
225ml double cream

Put the chocolate chip cookie crumbs in a bowl, add the cinnamon and melted butter, mix well and tip into a 22cm push-up-bottom or springform tin. Spread the mixture out evenly. Chill in the fridge until hard and set.

Melt the dark chocolate in a bain-marie (in a heatproof bowl over a pan of simmering water). Stir in the Kahlua or Tia Maria. Grate the white chocolate. Cut the vanilla pod in half lengthways, scrape out the seeds and add to the grated white chocolate.

Beat together the crème fraiche and demerara sugar until blended, then add the double cream and mix until smooth. Divide the mixture into 2 bowls. Add the melted dark chocolate and liqueur to the mixed creams in one bowl, and add the grated white chocolate and vanilla seeds to the other.

Spoon the two chocolate mixtures on to the chilled biscuit base and lightly mix with a fork to obtain a marbled effect. Chill for 3 hours before serving.

A truly special dessert: rich, dense and fragrant.
The marbled effect is easy to achieve, and for an
even more spectacular result, decorate with
chocolate curls or chocolate rose leaves.

Easy Chocolate Ice Cream

This grown-up chocolate ice cream, *Glâce 'Express' au Chocolat*, is from Janick Gestin of Laillé. Serve with your favourite toppings; chocolate curls, *crème Chantilly*, iced Kahlua or toasted almonds.

Preparation: 35 minutes
Freezing: 2 hours

Serves 6

150g dark or milk chocolate (70 per cent cocoa)
250ml milk
2 tbsp Kahlua liqueur
1 whole egg and 2 egg yolks
75g unrefined caster sugar
1 level tsp cornflour
350ml double cream

Break the chocolate into small pieces and place in a saucepan with the milk and Kahlua. Set over a low heat and stir until the chocolate has melted. Remove from the heat.

Place the egg and egg yolks with the sugar and cornflour in a heatproof bowl and beat until creamy and fluffy using an electric whisk. Pour in the melted chocolate and whisk well. Make a bain-marie and heat the mixture over a pan of simmering water, stirring constantly, until it begins to thicken (10–15 minutes). Remove from the heat and allow to cool a little.

Pour the cream into a bowl and whisk until it stands in soft peaks, then fold it into the chocolate mixture.

If you have an ice cream machine use it from here. If not, transfer the ice cream to a suitable container and leave in the freezer for 1 hour. Remove, beat the ice cream until smooth and return it to the freezer. Repeat until the ice cream has small crystals and can retain a good shape.

Chocolate Fondue

I love the informality of fondues and the picnic atmosphere they create. This sweet, light version is a perfect way to end a cheerful, noisy party. Use sweet almond oil if you can find it, but you can also make a good chocolate fondue without it.

Preparation: 25 minutes
Cooking: 15 minutes

Serves 6

For the fondue:
300g dark chocolate (70 per cent cocoa)
1 tbsp sweet almond oil, optional
100ml double cream
1 tbsp cognac

For dipping:
strawberries, apricot halves, pear slices, banana slices, peach slices, mandarin segments or small pieces of sponge cake

Break the chocolate into small pieces, put in a heatproof dish and melt in a bain-marie (over a pan of simmering water). Then add the oil, if using, the cream and cognac, and stir to make a glossy sauce for dipping. Transfer to a fondue bowl and keep warm with a night-light or burner. Serve the fondue at the table with dipping forks and all the dipping ingredients.

Chocolate Meringues

These luscious meringues are wonderful with *crème Chantilly* and fresh fruit.

Preparation: 15 minutes
Cooking: 2 hours

Serves 6

For the meringues:
3 egg whites
180g unrefined caster sugar
25g cocoa powder, sifted

For the *crème Chantilly*:
300ml whipping cream
25g unrefined caster sugar
1 tbsp Kahlua liqueur
chocolate (70 per cent cocoa) for decoration

Heat the oven to 140°C/gas 1.

Put the egg whites in a bowl and whisk rapidly until stiff, using an electric whisk if you have one. Add the caster sugar and whisk rapidly for another minute. Add the cocoa powder and whisk until blended.

Line a baking tray with baking parchment and scoop the meringue mixture on to the paper in 12 spoonfuls. Bake for 2 hours. For perfect crisp and dry meringues, turn the oven off but leave the meringues in there for another 12 hours.

Whisk the cream a little, add the sugar and Kahlua and continue to whisk carefully until it stands in soft peaks. Sandwich the meringues together with the Chantilly cream, and then, using a vegetable peeler, make chocolate curls and use them to decorate the meringues.

These beautiful meringues are a feature of many elegant French *pâtisseries*, like fluffy caramel-coloured clouds above the multicoloured fruit tarts and sculptural *pièces montées*.

Long before chocolate came to us from South America, the Aztecs drank an infusion of cacao spiced with pepper and chilli as part of their religious ceremonies. Later, as drinking chocolate gained popularity in Europe, sugar and milk were added to sweeten the bitter taste, and the strong spices were no longer needed to make it palatable.

Vianne's Spiced Hot Chocolate

Chilli may have lost favour as an ingredient in chocolate dishes in Europe, but for me this sweet, spiced version of hot chocolate is the best morning drink: rich, dark and invigorating enough to keep me going until lunchtime.

Preparation: 10 minutes
Cooking: 15 minutes

Serves 2

400ml full-fat milk
1/2 vanilla pod, cut in half lengthways
1/2 cinnamon stick
1 hot chilli, halved and deseeded
100g dark chocolate (70 per cent cocoa)
unrefined brown sugar to taste
whipped cream, chocolate curls, cognac or Amaretto to serve

Place the milk in a saucepan, add the vanilla pod, cinnamon stick and seedless chilli and gently bring it to a shivering simmer for 1 minute. Grate the chocolate and whisk it in until it melts. If you must, then add sugar, but do try it without. Take off the heat and allow it to infuse for 10 minutes, then remove the spices, return to the heat and bring gently back to simmering point. Serve in mugs topped with whipped cream, chocolate curls or a dash of cognac or Amaretto.

Index

Index of Recipe Titles

Conversion tables

Weights		Liquids		Oven temperatures		
5g	$^1/_4$ oz	15 ml	$^1/_2$ fl oz	110°C	225°F	gas mark $^1/_4$
15g	$^1/_2$ oz	25ml	1 fl oz	120°C	250°F	gas mark $^1/_2$
20g	$^3/_4$ oz	50ml	2 fl oz	140°C	275°F	gas mark 1
25g	1oz	75ml	3 fl oz	150°C	300°F	gas mark 2
50g	2oz	100ml	$3^1/_2$ fl oz	160°C	325°F	gas mark 3
75g	3oz	125ml	4 fl oz	180°C	350°F	gas mark 4
125g	4oz	150ml	$^1/_4$ pint	190°C	375°F	gas mark 5
150g	5oz	175ml	6 fl oz	200°C	400°F	gas mark 6
175g	6oz	200ml	7 fl oz	220°C	425°F	gas mark 7
200g	7oz	250ml	8 fl oz	230°C	450°F	gas mark 8
250g	8oz	275ml	9 fl oz	240°C	475°F	gas mark 9
275g	9oz	300ml	$^1/_2$ pint			
300g	10oz	325ml	11 fl oz			
325g	11oz	350ml	12 fl oz			
375g	12oz	375ml	13 fl oz			
400g	13oz	400ml	14 fl oz			
425g	14oz	450ml	$^3/_4$ pint			
475g	15oz	475ml	16 fl oz			
500g	1lb	500ml	17 fl oz			
625g	$1^1/_4$lb	550ml	18 fl oz			
750g	$1^1/_2$lb	600ml	1 pint			
875g	$1^3/_4$lb	750ml	$1^1/_4$ pints			
1kg	2 lb	900ml	$1^1/_2$ pints			
1.25kg	$2^1/_2$lb	1 litre	$1^3/_4$ pints			
1.5kg	3lb	1.2 litres	2 pints			
1.75kg	$3^1/_2$lb	1.5 litres	$2^1/_2$ pints			
2kg	4 lb	1.8 litres	3 pints			

Acknowledgements

The French kitchen is a sociable place where anybody can help out, whether they are doing the cooking, preparing the vegetables or simply telling stories to help the others pass the time. Heartfelt thanks to the many, many people who contributed ideas, recipes, photographs and all the other ingredients which make up this book; especially photographer Debi Treloar, designer Kenneth Carroll, jacket illustrator Stuart Haygarth and jacket designer Claire Ward, art director Liz Laczynska, editors Alison Tulett, Mari Roberts and Francesca Liversidge, and Warrior Maidens Serafina Clarke and Jennifer Luithlen. Thanks also to everyone who contributed ideas and recipes, including all the members of the Payen and Sorin families, Joanne's mother Jeannette Payen Short, Joanne's brother Lawrence, Jean and Simone Sorin, Claudine Pénisson, Denise Douazan and Mikaël Quaireau. Many thanks, too, to Marité and André Roty, Monique and Hamadi Kachkachi, Josette and Jacques Crochet, Juliette and Joseph Jeuland, Pierre and Janick Gestin, and Danielle and Michel Stéphan for all their help and their generous hospitality to our team during their stay in France.

We would like to thank Vicki Keppel-Compton and Laura Lenox Conyngham for recipe testing, and Vicki for assisting on the recipe shoot; Helen Trent for styling; and the following generous suppliers and hospitable hosts in both England and France.

The French House
78 York Street
London W1H 1DP
020 7298 6189
www.thefrench-house.com

M & C Vegetables
Turnham Green Terrace
London W4 1RG
020 8995 0140
www.m-and-c.co.uk

Mortimer and Bennet Deli
Turnham Green Terrace
London W4 1RG
020 8995 4145

Covent Garden Fishmongers
Turnham Green Terrace
London W4 1RG
020 8995 9273

Macken Brothers Butchers
Turnham Green Terrace
London W4 1RG
020 8994 2646

Farmers' markets everywhere: see www.farmersmarkets.net

Chalmers & Grey Fishmongers
67 Notting Hill Gate
London W11 3JS
020 7221 6177

Paul Bakery
115 Marylebone High Street
London W1U 4SB
020 7836 3304

Eurostar (UK) Limited
Waterloo Station
London SE1 8SE
08705 186 186
eurostar.com

Brittany Ferries
0870 5 360 360
www.brittanyferries.com

Aux Crus de Bourgogne
3 rue Bachaumont
75002 Paris
01 42 33 48 24

La Fromagerie 31
64 rue de Seine
75006 Paris
01 43 26 50 31

E. Dehillerin
18 et 20 rue Coquillière
75001 Paris
01 42 36 53 13

Hotel Aviatic
105 rue de Vaugirard
75006 Paris
01 53 63 25 50

Da Rosa
Epicurie Fine
62 rue de Seine
75006 Paris
01 40 51 00 09

Gerrard Judd
La Castafiore
51 rue St Louis en L'Île
75004 Paris

Segolene & Charles de Valbray
Château de Saint Patern
72610 Saint Patern
02 33 27 54 71
www.chateau-saintpaterne.com

Marquis et Marquise Gicquel des Touches
Château de Sarceaux
61250 Valframbert
02 33 28 85 11
www.chateauxcountry.com/chateaux/sarceaux

Joanne Harris and Fran Warde

Special Dedication

Given that my role in all this has been one of maximum enjoyment and minimum effort, I am donating my share of the proceeds to the humanitarian organization Médecins Sans Frontières, who are unique among aid charities in that they are entirely secular, non-judgemental and one hundred percent committed to helping the sick and the afflicted wherever they are and regardless of race, religion, or political affiliation. This book is dedicated to them, and to everyone who has not yet discovered the pleasures of their own kitchen - what are you waiting for?

Joanne Harris

Médecins Sans Frontières

Providing emergency medical relief to populations in danger

When an epidemic rages out of control, when a rain of shells reduces a town to ruins, when an area of conflict is too dangerous for most aid agencies to enter, MSF's skilled medical teams are there.

Médecins Sans Frontières (MSF) is the leading non-governmental organization for emergency medical aid. We provide independent medical relief to victims of war, disasters and epidemics in over eighty countries around the world, treating those who need it most, regardless of ethnic origin, religion or political affiliation.

Initially founded in Paris in 1971, MSF has become an international organization with support offices in 20 countries. Every year MSF sends around 2,500 volunteer doctors, nurses and technical support staff to some of the most far flung regions of the world to care for those most in need.

To get access to, and care for, those most vulnerable, MSF must remain scrupulously independent of governments as well as of religious and economic powers. We rely on private individuals for the majority of our funding.

You can contact us at:
Médecins Sans Frontières (UK)
67-74 Saffron Hill
London EC1N 8QX

Tel: 020 7404 6600
Fax: 020 7404 4466
e-mail: office-ldn@london.msf.org
website: www.uk.msf.org